Sacred Narratives: The Literary Craft of the Bible

R. M. Shepherd

ISBN: 979-8-9923341-2-8 (softcover)

"Scripture taken from the NEW AMERICAN STANDARD BIBLE, Copyright © 1960, 1962, 1963, 1971, 1972, 1973, 1975, 1977, 1995, by The Lockman Foundation.   Used by permission."

Book Cover Photo by StockSnap. Used by permission.

Printed in the United States of America.

Publisher: Indy Pub

Special thanks to Richard and Barbara for their comments during development of this topic.

About the Author

R. M. Shepherd, JD, PhD, received theological training at Trinity Theological Seminary. Shepherd believes that understanding the Bible's various literary genres is an aid to interpreting its content. The theology of John Knox, a preacher prominent in the English Reformation's early years, is explored in her book *Sounding God's Trumpet*. She's also the author of several historical fiction novels.

Contents

Introduction

Welcome to *Sacred Narratives: The Literary Craft of the Bible.* This book approaches the Bible as a literary work, enhancing students' appreciation of the people, cultures, and messages contained within its pages. By engaging with the text as literature, we will explore a variety of literary techniques and how the authors of the Bible employ them.

The book comprises five chapters that help you better understand the material. The first chapter will focus on Old Testament narratives and the core principles of storytelling. In the second chapter, we will explore the intricate world of poetry and wisdom literature. In chapter three, we'll go through the Gospels and see how Jesus taught his disciples and the crowds. Next, we'll talk about the early church by reviewing Acts and the Letters in the fourth chapter. The last chapter is about visionary literature. It looks at prophecies from the Old Testament prophets, Jesus, and the Book of Revelation.

You may ask, "Doesn't this suggest that the Bible is fictional?" Regarding it as literature doesn't mean it's fictional, although authors sometimes use fiction as a narrative technique. The acknowledgment of the Bible as a literary piece does not undermine the notion that God inspired its authors.

All Scripture is inspired by God and profitable for teaching, for reproof, for correction, for training in righteousness; so that the [people] of God may be adequate, equipped for every good work.[1] 2 Timothy 3:16–17.

In past centuries, when few could read and write, humanity depended on the craft of verbal storytelling to convey knowledge, using established narrative conventions. The Bible contains many genres:

- History, biography, and other types of storytelling.

- Poetry, which is found in the book of Psalms, but also as praise songs, worship songs, and lamentations (expressions of sorrow or grief) in other books.

- Wisdom literature, such as Proverbs, Ecclesiastes, and Job.

- The Gospels which include short stories and parables. Narratives tell the story of Jesus, focusing on His ministry and passion. He used parables as a teaching method, incorporating imagery and coded messages.

- The Book of Acts and the letters by various authors seek to provide direction and inspiration for the new churches.

- Visionary literature, which includes prophetic and apocalyptic visions.

This overview does not offer an exhaustive treatment of literary techniques and how they appear in the Bible. The goal is to acquaint the participant with this approach of interpreting the Bible to nurture a closer connection with God. Many scholars engage in a thorough analysis of literary techniques. Two books that guided this effort are *How to Read the Bible for All Its Worth* by Gordon D. Fee and Douglas K. Stuart, [2] and *How to Read the Bible as Literature* by Leland Ryken. [3]

Settings and Dialog

When analyzing a story, it helps to pay attention to settings. Location may contribute to the plot by acting as the source of the conflict, such as a drought or a raging sea. A field or vineyard filled with ripe crops will arouse different emotions in the audience than a battlefield filled with corpses. Culture, customs, and period impact the story's theme.

Dialog slows the pace of the plot, alerting the reader to pay attention. Dialog exposes various character traits, like patience, kindness, or anger. The beginning of a dialog provides clues to what is important to the narrator. Dialog between two characters may show a contrast between them and give the reader more insight into the motives of the character. Sometimes, one character will repeat or summarize the crucial part of a statement to provide emphasis.

Symbols and Imagery

Being conscious of symbols and imagery is crucial as they convey significant information with minimal words. Symbols have a literal meaning but suggest a different meaning. Sometimes, symbols served as a code to communicate with other Jews without the Gentiles understanding their meaning. Images use a vivid description to appeal to the reader's senses. Here are some examples.

- The Garden of Eden is a symbol of perfection. God created it and humans lived there in the beginning. Abundance of food, life, health, and perfect harmony in nature prevailed. Being expelled from the Garden symbolizes loss of innocence and the beginning of danger, labor, illness, and death. Genesis describes the original Garden, and Revelation describes a new Garden that repeats many images of the original one.

- The Promised Land was an area God set aside for the Hebrews as a safe and prosperous place to live in obedience to Him. It contrasted with Egypt, where the Hebrews suffered as slaves.

The Jews attributed special meaning to numbers. Listed below are some examples.

- The number twelve represents the twelve tribes of Israel. Jesus further emphasizes this significance by appointing twelve apostles.

- According to biblical accounts, God took seven days to create the heavens and the earth. The number seven recurs throughout the Bible. Revelation features seven trumpets, plagues, and churches. Sacrifices often included seven lambs or seven bulls.

- Another number is four. The four winds and the four corners of the earth symbolize completion or fullness. The number forty suggests transition or change, such as the Hebrews spent forty years in the wilderness, while Jesus spent forty days in the wilderness.

- Moses appointed seventy elders to help him settle disputes. Psalm 90 refers to seventy years as our normal life span. The Jews were in exile in Babylon for seventy years. Jesus combined seven and seventy by saying we should forgive seventy times seven.

- As an agrarian society, the people understood the meaning of roots and their importance for a plant to grow. Roots or stumps represented ancestors, while branches, fruit, or stems represented descendants. They drew the distinction that bad roots produced bad fruit, while good roots produced good fruit.

- Water is a recurrent symbol. In Genesis, the sea stands for chaos. Later, God directs Moses to produce water from rocks in the desert. The Jews crossed the Jordan River to enter the Promised Land. Jesus claimed to be the living water during His encounter with the Samaritan woman at Jacob's well. Jonah embarked on a ship to escape from God, but when a powerful storm jeopardized the vessel, the sailors threw him into the sea, and a large fish swallowed him.

Many literary techniques appear in the narratives. Understanding the technique will point to clues to understanding the Bible. Chapter one involves analysis of the Old Testament Narratives.

---

1. All Scripture references are from the New American Standard Bible (NASB): 1995 Update (La Habra, CA: The Lockman Foundation, 1995).

2. Gordon D. Fee and Douglas K. Stuart, *How to Read the Bible for all its Worth*, 3 ed. (Grand Rapids, MI: Zondervan, 2003).

3. Leland Ryken, *How to Read the Bible as Literature*, (Grand Rapids, MI: Zondervan, 1984).

Chapter One

Old Testament Narratives

This chapter focuses on the narrative techniques used in the Old Testament. In addition to a review of the narrative levels of the Bible, we will see how narrative and character arcs build the foundations of the story. We will analyze the pyramid structure used by many storytellers. To see how the phases of the story structure apply, we will analyze stories of Joseph and Ruth.

Three Narrative Levels

One way to look at the Bible is to recognize three narrative levels. [1] The top level (meta-narrative) is God's plan for Creation. It starts in Genesis with the Creation story when Adam and Eve dwell in the Garden of Eden. The overall story arc of the Bible features God as the protagonist. Evil people or powers (sometimes Satan) are the antagonists. The section below covers the topic of characters and narrators in more depth.

God's redemptive plan, starting with the first covenant made with the chosen people, is part of the middle level. At this level, each story has its own protagonist taking center stage. For example, Abraham becomes the father of a prosperous nation known as Israel. Following the enslavement of the Jews in Egypt, Moses becomes the protagonist involved in their liberation and journey to the Promised Land. As the narrative progresses, the reader encounters a continuous stream of judges and kings, each contributing to the overall storyline.

The bottom level has shorter stories about individuals and their successes and failures when living as God's chosen people. Examples are Abraham, Moses, Joshua, King David, King Solomon, and Elisha. The narratives cover several millennia, recounting the struggles, successes, and failures of God's chosen people. While humans fail frequently, God is unfailing as He offers forgiveness and redemption to us. The Bible speaks of hope and a promise from God and Jesus to restore the world to its original perfection.

This chapter looks at the Pentateuch and the histories in the Old Testament. The Pentateuch refers to the first five books of the Bible. Genesis begins with the story of Creation and Adam and Eve and their children. It continues with the descendants of the first couple, their struggles with sinfulness, and their acts of faith and obedience.

The covenant with Abraham tells us that God pronounces Abraham righteous, promises he will be the father of a prosperous nation, and foretells that his descendant will bring redemption to humankind.

Exodus through Deuteronomy describes the enslavement of the Hebrews in Egypt, their escape when God sends Moses to confront the Pharaoh, and the forty years in the wilderness during which they receive the Law and the Ten Commandments.

In these histories, the narrative shifts to the Jews entering the Promised Land. God elevates judges to lead the chosen people after Moses died. After the Jews pleaded for a king, God agreed to anoint a king to lead them. Despite frequent warnings from God, they worship pagan idols and adopt pagan practices, as they cannot obey God. Israel split into the kingdoms of Israel and Judah after King Solomon died.

First Assyria conquered Israel, then Babylon conquered Judah, and destroyed the Temple in Jerusalem. Many Jews went into exile in Babylon

(597-538 BCE) and enslavement. After they regained their freedom and returned to Israel and Judah, they committed themselves to rebuilding the Temple and reviving their religious traditions.

Story Structure

Stories have a beginning, a middle, and an end. Narration uses the term story arc to describe the structure of a story. Narratives include characters, a catalyst, conflict, and resolution. There's either a purpose or a promise present. Characters may also have an arc describing how they resolve conflicts and learn valuable lessons during the story.

When the events in the Bible happened, most people couldn't read and there was a shortage of writing materials. To convey the information, a speaker recited these stories to an audience. So, instead of using italics, bold fonts, or punctuation, the storyteller used other techniques.

Not all narratives in the Old Testament teach a moral lesson for us to follow. They are about what God did regarding the Jews. For example, the central theme of the story of Jacob and Esau pertains to the Jews tracing their ancestry back to Jacob, not parental favoritism among siblings.

While the plots are basic, the writer sometimes incorporates subplots. A subplot may interrupt the plot, then the main plot reemerges. For example, in the story of Abraham, subplots emerge involving Lot, Rebekah, and Hagar and Ishmael.

Mirroring or inclusion is another technique used by the narrator. In Joseph's story, his brothers bow to him in a dream in Genesis 37, then in real life in Genesis 50. Deuteronomy's narratives have an A B C B A pattern. [2] The narrator uses repetition to emphasize the point.

The narrator may be one character in the story telling what they experienced (first person point of view or POV). They only share what they see or hear firsthand. A detached observer who has more information than the characters can adopt the third person POV.

Bible narrators often omit physical descriptions of the characters, preferring instead to emphasize their wealth, social status, occupation, or tribal affiliation. Even if people do not acknowledge God, He remains the protagonist. The characters' actions reveal God's guidance and plan, culminating in a positive result.

Character Arc

A character arc occurs when a character experiences an internal transformation while confronting conflict. A narrative contains two primary character arcs, although there may be more. Character arcs happen apart from the story arcs. The contrasting arcs of characters generate tension and suspense.

- Protagonist (this is the hero/heroine). The main character shows change and growth during the story. The change can be either positive or negative.

- Antagonist (this could be the villain). A character or force which seeks to block the hero from reaching their goals. The hero must discover a way to thwart the villain.

- Supporting characters have their own arcs, distinct from the protagonist's arc.

Through the narrative, we see the characters' strengths and weaknesses. The protagonists react to a catalyst and go into action. The villain may be the catalyst or could be a force impeding the hero. Heroes, although flawed, learn important moral and spiritual lessons. The villain appears to defeat the hero, but in the end suffers defeat. What differs in the Bible is God's grace and mercy which rescue the flawed character.

Hero Arc

Let's look at some examples. The Hero/Heroine Arc can be a male or female. The problem to resolve may be internal (heroine) or external (hero), and can be a combination of both. In Exodus, Pharaoh's daughter rescued baby Moses from the Nile, marking the beginning of his narrative. In his next appearance as a young man, he killed an Egyptian soldier who beat a Hebrew worker. Pharaoh sought to kill Moses, which triggered his flight to the desert of Midian, where he would herd sheep for forty years.

God directed Moses to return to Egypt to demand Pharaoh free the Hebrews from their enslavement. Moses resisted, but eventually returned to Egypt with his brother Aaron. He chose obedience to God, and God gave him power to perform miracles astounding the court magicians.

The narrative explains how Moses, despite his fear, anxiety, and speech disability, confronted Pharaoh. After the Egyptians suffered a series of plagues, Pharoah released the Hebrews. Moses then led the rebellious Hebrews in the wilderness for forty years until God allowed them to enter the Promised Land.

Moses faced an external conflict because the Pharaoh refused to release the Hebrews. Egyptians regarded them with disdain. The Hebrews were afraid of the unknown and resisted Moses as well. His internal conflicts were his lack of self-confidence and his fear of arrest or execution. During that time, Moses made mistakes but always relied on God. He learned lessons contributing to his moral and spiritual growth.

Villain Arc

The antagonist, also known as the Villain, can be a person or a force. In Genesis, Jacob left his home to live with his Uncle Laban in Paddan-Aran where he fell in love with the younger daughter Rachel. He struck a bargain with Laban, trading seven years of labor for Rachel's hand in marriage. At the marriage, the bride wore a heavy veil. After spending the night together, Jacob discovered he had married Leah, her older sister. Jacob protested, but Laban offered Rachel in exchange for another seven years of labor. After the additional seven years, Jacob had no property of his own. He negotiated with Laban to gain a herd based on the coloration of the animals. Despite Laban's repeated changes to the terms of the agreement, Jacob's herds prospered. When Laban became angry, God warned Jacob to leave secretly with his family, servants, and herds.

Despite Laban's warm greeting, he was dishonest and took advantage of Jacob in their relationship. His external conflict was he needed to have Leah marry. He tricked Jacob by substituting Leah at the wedding. To gain Rachel, Jacob had to work twice as long as the original agreement. Laban's inner struggle stemmed from his dishonesty, leading to a constant reliance on deception. Jacob's prosperity as a shepherd, blessed by God, filled Laban with jealousy. Jacob's departure with his family finally thwarted Laban's plans.

Story Arcs

Let's turn to narrative arcs in the Old Testament. Because of its widespread recognition, we will use the pyramid model to analyze two stories. Here we show the stages of a story: exposition, catalyst, rising action, climax, falling action, and resolution. Let's look at each stage in greater depth.

The first stage is **Exposition**, which provides the background, the setting, and introduces the main characters to the audience. It may introduce the conflict or problem to be solved.

The **Catalyst** is a problem that forces the hero to act. Solving the problem requires them to step out of their comfort zone.

Rising action details the actions of the hero, and the friends who help along the way. The villain attempts to hinder the hero. To heighten the tension, the hero might experiment with different solutions that result in failure. The antagonist seems to win the conflict. Tension builds to the next stage.

The **Climax** to the story is a turning point, usually when the hero understands the solution to the problem. It may be the midpoint of the story, or it could be close to the end.

Falling action occurs on the other side of the pyramid. The hero implements the solution and thwarts the antagonist.

The **Resolution** describes what it looks like with the problem resolved, and what the hero's life becomes.

Look at these two examples of the story arcs.

The first story from Genesis features a self-indulgent and haughty youth who is the eleventh of twelve sons. The setting starts in Hebron but mainly takes place in Egypt.

Exposition: According to the narrative, Joseph's father favored him by granting him a special coat and other privileges while his brothers toiled in the fields. It angered the brothers to listen to him brag about his dreams and his claims regarding future superiority over them.

Catalyst: The brothers plotted to kill Joseph, but Judah, the oldest, convinced them to sell him to Midianites going to Egypt. The brothers lied to Jacob and told him that a wild animal had killed their brother.

Rising action: In Egypt, Joseph served as a slave in Potiphar's house. He showed moral courage by refusing to sleep with his master's wife, leading to his imprisonment after her false accusation. He showed integrity in assisting the jailer who recommended him to Pharoah.

Climax: Joseph interpreted Pharaoh's dreams of famine with accuracy. Pharoah elevated him to a powerful position in Egypt. As a result, Egypt stockpiled food to prepare for the impending famine.

Falling action: His older brothers arrived in Egypt and pleaded for help during the famine. They did not recognize him, but he recognized them. His father, Jacob, and younger brother, Benjamin, remained in Hebron.

Joseph tricked his brothers into bringing Benjamin to Egypt. Joseph put his cup in Benjamin's sack of food, then had him arrested for theft after the brothers left the city. He vowed to keep Benjamin as his slave and let the other brothers leave. Judah protested it would kill his father and offered to stay in his place.

Resolution: Joseph revealed his identity. He and his brothers reconciled, and he reunited with his father who believed him to be dead. The Hebrews moved to Egypt. They prospered and flourished because of the generous provision of food and land by the Egyptians. This story explains the presence of Jacob's descendants in Egypt.

The next story is not as dramatic, but is important to Jewish history. It tells the story of Ruth, an ancestor of Jesus. Two laws play a significant role in this story. The law of gleaning permitted Ruth, a poor foreigner, to harvest leftover grain from Boaz's fields (Leviticus 19:9–10). The other law is that of the kinsman redeemer (Leviticus 25:47-55). Naomi's husband sold his land in Bethlehem when he moved to Moab. After he and both sons died,

Boaz had the right to redeem the land, as he was a kinsman. However, the kinsman redeemer was responsible for marrying the deceased man's widow and having children who would inherit the land. [3]

Ruth lived during the time of the Judges. This story is about God's kindness, and the kindness of Ruth, Naomi, and Boaz. Although Ruth and Boaz's relationship is significant, romance is not the focus of the story.

During Moses' time, the Moabite women lured the Hebrews into immorality and idolatry. This story instead shows a Moabite woman converting to Judaism and living according to their laws.

Exposition: Because of a famine in Bethlehem, Naomi's husband sold his land and moved the family to Moab, where they lived about ten years. Ruth, a Moabitess, married one son while another Moabitess married the other son. Ruth converted to Judaism.

Catalyst: Naomi's husband and both sons died, leaving her and the daughters-in-law widows without a means of support. Moab suffered from a severe famine. Naomi headed back to Bethlehem in Judah, and Ruth went with her.

Rising action: Ruth went into the fields to glean so they could eat. She met Boaz, a wealthy relative of Naomi's husband. He urged Ruth to glean in his fields and drink water from his wells. Eventually, he invited her to eat with the reapers. He acknowledged her kindness towards Naomi.

Climax: Naomi instructed Ruth to "lay" at Boaz's feet, setting the stage for him to redeem (marry) her. Ruth readied herself to meet Boaz, in the same way a bride would prepare for her wedding. [4] She washed, anointed herself with fragrant oil, and put on her best clothes. Boaz was willing, but he was aware the claim of a closer kinsman to Naomi's husband was superior. He agreed to purchase the land and marry her, providing the man did not wish to do so.

Falling action: Boaz met with the other man, who declined to redeem her.

Resolution: Boaz married Ruth and bought the land for her children. This ensured that she and Naomi were no longer poor, and she was no longer a widow. Boaz and Ruth were parents of Obed, father of Jesse, father of David, and ancestor of Jesus.

———————◆O◆———————

To summarize, we learned about genres in the Bible. Focusing on Old Testament narratives, we identified some of the important features in a story, such as location, dialog, and symbols. We analyzed how narrative and character arcs build the foundations of the story. We reviewed the pyramid structure used by many storytellers. Then we analyzed two stories to see how the phases of the story structure applied to them.

I hope that by understanding these factors, you will appreciate the literary craft of the storytellers more.

In Chapter Two, we will explore the presentation of poetic forms and wisdom literature in the Bible.

---

1. Fee, 91.

2. Fee, 98.

3. Warren W. Wiersbe, *Be Committed*, "Be" Commentary Series (Wheaton, Il: Victor Books, 1993), 37–38.

4. Wiersbe, *Be Committed*, 40.

Poetry and Wisdom Literature

I n this chapter, we will explore a different literary form, focusing on the Psalms and wisdom books. Poetry serves as a condensed method for transmitting information. Mnemonic devices, such as acrostics, rhyming, and music, make it easier to remember a poem compared to prose.

Collections of songs and poems from 1000 to 800 BCE comprise books of poetry and wisdom literature. The book of Psalms holds immense religious and cultural importance. Composed over a period of several centuries, various authors wrote the psalms, including David and Solomon. Scholars believe that the prophet Jeremiah wrote the book of Lamentations, which showcases Hebrew poetry. Proverbs, Ecclesiastes, Song of Solomon, and Job, the books of wisdom, include poetry as well.

Psalms

The book of Psalms contains one hundred and fifty individual psalms, each with its own unique style and theme. These psalms express a broad spectrum of emotions, including joy, praise, anger, lament, and sorrow. They explore themes of faith, gratitude, hope, and the human condition in relation to God. The Psalms serve as a guide for worship, prayer, and spiritual reflection for believers of different faith traditions. People have recited, sung, and studied many of these poetic verses and songs throughout history.

If you are familiar with modern poetry, you will spot differences in Biblical poetry. Rhyming and rhythm are common elements in modern poetry. In contrast, Biblical poetry uses techniques such as parallelism and repetition to emphasize ideas. Just like modern poetry, it uses figurative language such as imagery, similes, and metaphors to evoke a reaction from the reader. Images can captivate and stimulate the senses. The reader can see, hear, feel, or taste the elements in the description. Later, we will discuss other techniques.

Psalm 1:1-6 showcases parallelism, imagery, and figurative language. Lines occur in twos or threes.

How blessed is the man who does not walk in the counsel of the wicked, Nor stand in the path of sinners, Nor sit in the seat of scoffers!

But his delight is in the law of the Lord, And in His law he meditates day and night.

The wicked are not so, But they are like chaff which the wind drives away.

Therefore the wicked will not stand in the judgment, Nor sinners in the assembly of the righteous.

For the Lord knows the way of the righteous, But the way of the wicked will perish.

In verse 1, the poet describes three negative actions: *"not walk," "nor stand,"* and *"nor sit."* The first three lines repeated the same theme: *"the wicked," "sinners,"* and *"scoffers."* Verse 2 reversed the negative statements by emphasizing *"his delight is in the law"* and *"in His law he meditates."* Verses 4-6 return to a description of consequences for *"the wicked."*

Simile and Metaphor

Figurative language includes simile and metaphor. A simile uses the words "like" or "as" to compare two objects. Psalm 1 features a tree and a stream in its imagery. This evokes a pastoral atmosphere for the reader. The reader can feel the wind and see the chaff disappear. The sturdy tree with deep roots contrasts with the transient nature of chaff. Again, we look at Psalm 1:3-4.

He will be like a tree firmly planted by streams of water ...

The wicked are not so, But they are like chaff which the wind drives away.

Referring to the man as *"like a tree"* is a simile. This is not a physical description but points out aspects of his character that have the positive qualities of a tree. He describes wicked people as inconsequential, like chaff, able to be blown away by a breeze. The poet is comparing their character to something fleeting. The verses below are metaphors.

How blessed is the man who does not walk in the counsel of the wicked, Nor stand in the path of sinners, Nor sit in the seat of scoffers! Psalm 1:1

He guides me in the paths of righteousness ... Psalm 23:3

A metaphor is a direct comparison. Psalm 1 uses the phrase *"walk in the counsel of the wicked...."* When we talk about counsel, we mean guidance, not a physical space to walk into. Also, *"path of sinners"* is not a physical path or road with that title. A place of assembly would not have seating labeled as *"scoffers."* Psalm 23 uses the metaphor *"paths of righteousness ..."* which is not a physical path.

Psalm 42:1-4a is another example of the use of metaphor.

As the deer pants for the water brooks,

So my soul pants for You, O God.

My soul thirsts for God, for the living God;

When shall I come and appear before God?

My tears have been my food day and night,

While they say to me all day long, "Where is your God?"

These things I remember and I pour out my soul within me.

The phrase "...*so my soul pants...*" and *"My soul thirsts..."* are metaphors. Verse 1 draws a connection between a thirsty deer seeking water, and a thirsty soul seeking God. Another metaphor is *"My tears have been my food...."* This implies the poet has not eaten regular food but has wept instead. Another phrase is *"I pour out my soul,"* comparing the soul to liquid.

Poetic license

The term poetic license refers to the improbable statements made by poets. Here are some examples.

In Psalm 1:2, the man *"...meditates day and night."* It is impossible because the man must stop for sleep, food, and other essential activities to live. One interpretation of this is that it happens both morning and evening, but not all day and all night.

But his delight is in the law of the Lord, And in His law he meditates day and night. Psalm 1:2

Psalm 23 contains poetic license techniques. The first phrase, *"The Lord is my shepherd...,"* makes an improbable statement. It portrays God as a person tending to a flock of sheep. During that era, shepherds held a low social status, taking part in activities centered on the fields. Still, sheep were important to the economy, and without the shepherd, the flock would become prey for wild animals. Other dangers to the animals include injury and lack of nourishment. To Jews, the shepherd symbolized a vigilant guardian, defending and providing sustenance for his flock. As you read this poem, you can imagine the picturesque landscapes of verdant pastures and serene bodies of water that it describes.

By using figurative language, the poet depicted a path or roadway in the third verse. Righteous wasn't the name or destination of any physical path.

Death does not cast a shadow.

The Lord is my shepherd, I shall not want. Psalm 23:1

... He guides me in the paths of righteousness For His name's sake.

Even though I walk through the valley of the shadow of death, ... Psalm 23:3-4

Another example is Psalm 42:7. The writer could not have visited all the oceans and bodies of water to experience this. Still, anyone who has experienced relentless waves pounding against them can comprehend the profound fear and overwhelming feeling of helplessness that causes.

... All Your breakers and Your waves have rolled over me. Psalm 42:7

Apostrophe

Writers use the term "Apostrophe" when they talk to someone who is not present, or even an inanimate object. This is a literary technique used to generate excitement or intensity. For example, in Psalm 23:1-3, the writer refers to God as He or His, but in verses 4-5, the poet switches to You or Your, speaking to God directly.

The Lord is my shepherd, I shall not want.

He makes me lie down in green pastures; He leads me beside quiet waters.

He restores my soul; He guides me in the paths of righteousness For His name's sake.

Even though I walk through the valley of the shadow of death, I fear no evil, for You are with me; Your rod and Your staff, they comfort me.

You prepare a table before me in the presence of my enemies; You have anointed my head with oil;

My cup overflows. Psalm 23:1-5

Here are other examples of apostrophe. In Psalm 42:7, the poet is talking to gates as though they have not only a head to lift, but ears to hear. And in Psalm 103:1-2, the poet talks to his soul.

Lift up your heads, O gates, And be lifted up, O ancient doors, That the King of glory may come in! Psalm 42:7

Bless the Lord, O my soul, And all that is within me, bless His holy name. Bless the Lord, O my soul, And forget none of His benefits; .... Psalm 103:1-2

Imprecatory psalms

The imprecatory psalms express anger and seek revenge on the author's enemies. They contain prayers or requests to God for justice, retribution, or penalties towards adversaries or oppressors. The poet expresses feelings of anger, frustration, or injustice. They seek God's intervention to bring justice and deliverance. Often written in times of conflict, oppression, or persecution, the imprecatory psalms convey intense emotions and desperate appeals for God's aid.

Here is an example of an imprecatory psalm. On multiple occasions, enemies pursued David, aiming to end his life. He composed Psalm 35 to ask God for His protection. Review the verses below.

Let those be ashamed and dishonored who seek my life;
Let those be turned back and humiliated who devise evil against me.
Let them be like chaff before the wind,
With the angel of the Lord driving them on.
Let their way be dark and slippery,
With the angel of the Lord pursuing them.
For without cause they hid their net for me;
Without cause they dug a pit for my soul.
Let destruction come upon him unawares,
And let the net which he hid catch himself;
Into that very destruction let him fall. Psalm 35:4-8

The repetition of the word "*Let*" requests God to act against his enemies. Like Psalm 1, it compares the wicked and chaff, which is blown away by God. Another torment directed at his enemies is a dark slippery path with an angel pursuing them. He began by calling for their dishonor, but progressed to calling for their destruction.

David also wrote Psalm 69. In this excerpt of verses 22-28, his anger is clear from his choice of torments. He implores God to trap his enemies like an animal and to inflict them with blindness, death, and being removed from the Book of Life. He refers to himself in the third person as the one " *whom You have wounded.*" This psalm repeats the word "may" as a request for God to act.

May their table before them become a snare;
And when they are in peace, may it become a trap.
May their eyes grow dim so that they cannot see,
And make their loins shake continually.
Pour out Your indignation on them,
And may Your burning anger overtake them.
May their camp be desolate;
May none dwell in their tents.
For they have persecuted him whom You Yourself have smitten,
And they tell of the pain of those whom You have wounded.
Add iniquity to their iniquity,
And may they not come into Your righteousness.
May they be blotted out of the book of life
And may they not be recorded with the righteous. Psalm 69:22-28.

Lamentations

Now we will look at Lamentations. It uses some different literary techniques than we have reviewed so far. After the Babylonians destroyed Jerusalem and carried many of its inhabitants into exile, a poet believed to be Jeremiah wrote Lamentations. It uses repetition of thought in couplets or triplets for its poetic rhythm. These lines support or elaborate on the same idea or provide a different viewpoint.

Jeremiah employed acrostics as another technique, starting each line with successive letters of the Hebrew alphabet. The modern reader would not notice this without knowing Hebrew.

Five chapters comprise this book, including four dirges and a prayer. A dirge is a mournful song, piece of music, or poem. In Chapter 1, the author depicts Jerusalem as a grieving widow. Chapter 2 describes the Jews as a people punished by God. Chapter 3 is more personal in which Jeremiah details his suffering and promises repentance.

In Lamentations 1:1-2, the poet uses simile and metaphor, comparing Jerusalem to a princess, a widow, and a laborer. He uses a metaphor when he writes the city weeps and has tears on her cheeks. References to lovers, friends, and enemies continue this personification.

How lonely sits the city That was full of people!
She has become like a widow Who was once great among the nations!
She who was a princess among the provinces Has become a forced laborer!
She weeps bitterly in the night And her tears are on her cheeks;
She has none to comfort her Among all her lovers.
All her friends have dealt treacherously with her;
They have become her enemies. Lamentations 1:1-2

This also refers to the spiritual loss suffered by the city. Sacrifices and festivals were canceled due to the Temple's absence. Once a city admired for its wealth, it became impoverished.

The third chapter turns from the city to the poet himself and what God did to him. The author uses three similes to paint a picture of God as a mighty bear or lion, while comparing himself to a helpless target.

He is to me like a bear lying in wait,

Like a lion in secret places.

He has turned aside my ways and torn me to pieces;

He has made me desolate.

He bent His bow

And set me as a target for the arrow. Lamentations 3:10-12

Despite his feelings of persecution, the poet still expresses his faith in God's steadfastness in Lamentations 3:22-23. He amplifies *"never cease"* with *"never fail"* and *"new every morning."* He switches from addressing God in the third person with *"His compassions"* to the second person *"Your faithfulness."*

The Lord's loving-kindnesses indeed never cease,

For His compassions never fail.

They are new every morning;

Great is Your faithfulness. Lamentations 3:22-23

Lamentations Chapter 5 differs from the preceding chapters because it does not use acrostic.

You, O Lord, rule forever; Your throne is from generation to generation.

Why do You forget us forever? Why do You forsake us so long?

Restore us to You, O Lord, that we may be restored; Renew our days as of old,

Unless You have utterly rejected us And are exceedingly angry with us. Lamentations 5:19–22

Each stanza comprises a single line. The initial line expands upon *"rule forever"* by adding *"from generation to generation."* The next line uses the phrases *"forget us"* and *"forsake us."* *"Restore"* is repeated in the third line along with the addition of *"renew."* *"[R]ejected us"* and *"angry with us"* is in the last one. In a plea for guidance, the author seeks answers from God while simultaneously declaring his unwavering devotion.

Wisdom literature

Let's now direct our attention to wisdom literature. The primary aim of wisdom literature is to make godly choices. It offers practical guidance on how to navigate the difficulties that arise in our everyday lives, while emphasizing the importance of aligning our actions with God's will. Wisdom books use the same techniques as poetry.

Wisdom literature includes Proverbs and Ecclesiastes, written by Solomon. Solomon asked God for the gift of wisdom after David died. God granted his request, and his wise decisions became well known. The uniqueness of Song of Songs, also called Song of Solomon, lies in its blend of wisdom and poetic expression.

Job is also part of wisdom literature. Job suffers loss, and the book is a debate between him and his friends about whether God was punishing him for wrongdoing.

Proverbs

We will first turn our attention to the book of Proverbs. The advice in Proverbs is practical and easy to remember. Proverbs use poetic techniques to evoke a stronger reaction from readers. For example, Proverbs 3:5-6 uses figurative language in a concise warning against assuming greater knowledge or solutions than God possesses.

Trust in the Lord with all your heart
And do not lean on your own understanding.
In all your ways acknowledge Him,
And He will make your paths straight. Proverbs 3:5-6

People today believe trust is in the mind, not the heart. Understanding is not a physical structure that will support weight. It does not mean that one will never encounter a curve in the road.

It is customary for proverbs to be expressed in just two phrases or sentences. Sometimes the word "but" separates the thoughts to contrast two ideas. While brief, their meaning runs deep. For instance, here is Proverbs 15:1.

A gentle answer turns away wrath,
But a harsh word stirs up anger.

How often do we hear stories of minor disagreements spiraling into violence because of the exchange of harsh words?

Another is Proverbs 15:12.

A scoffer does not love one who reproves him,
He will not go to the wise. Proverbs 15:12

Individuals with little knowledge may think they know more than they do and ignore the insights of experts.

Many people agree Proverbs 16:9 is an undeniable truth. It's common to hear people talk about their plans being disrupted by unforeseen circumstances, leading them to pursue a different path.

The mind of man plans his way,
But the Lord directs his steps. Proverbs 16:9

Ecclesiastes

Now we will turn to Ecclesiastes. Reading Ecclesiastes requires understanding the context and not extracting verses in isolation. The text occasionally takes on a cynical tone. The author has four key themes: [1]

1. Only God creates and gives life.

2. God's ways are beyond human comprehension.

3. Appearances can be deceiving.

4. Death is inevitable for everyone.

In Ecclesiastes, phrases like *"under the sun"* suggest negativity, while *" above the sun"* implies positivity. Rather than a grim or discouraging statement, it reminds the reader that some pursuits may not bring satisfaction. Ecclesiastes 1:2 leads with a caution against vanity.

'Vanity of vanities,' says the Preacher, 'Vanity of vanities! All is vanity.'

A few chapters later, the author repeats the theme that God's ways are unknowable. In Ecclesiastes 7:16-18, there is a warning against being overly self-righteous or relying too much on one's own wisdom, as it can lead to arrogance and self-deception.

Do not be excessively wicked and do not be a fool. Why should you die before your time?

It is good that you grasp one thing and also not let go of the other; for the one who fears God comes forth with both of them. Ecclesiastes 7:16-18

Ecclesiastes 3:1-8 reflects upon the cycles of life and suggests that things happen at their appropriate time, such as sowing seeds and reaping the crops they produce. In this passage, wisdom comes from accepting life's natural changes. By repeating *"A time to..."* the author establishes a rhythm.

There is an appointed time for everything. And there is a time for every event under heaven—

A time to give birth and a time to die;

A time to plant and a time to uproot what is planted.

A time to kill and a time to heal;

A time to tear down and a time to build up.

A time to weep and a time to laugh;

A time to mourn and a time to dance.

A time to throw stones and a time to gather stones;

A time to embrace and a time to shun embracing.

A time to search and a time to give up as lost;

A time to keep and a time to throw away.

A time to tear apart and a time to sew together;

A time to be silent and a time to speak.

A time to love and a time to hate;

A time for war and a time for peace. Ecclesiastes 3:1-8

The book concludes with the admonition to fear God and keep His commandments, as the whole duty of humankind is to follow God's will. The word "fear" in this instance means to give God reverence and respect. Life is about the journey, not the destination.

The conclusion, when all has been heard, is: fear God and keep His commandments, because this applies to every person. For God will bring every act to judgment, everything which is hidden, whether it is good or evil. Ecclesiastes 12:13-14

Job

The next book of wisdom we will analyze is Job. This book emphasizes that life isn't fair and that unfortunate events are not always punishment for someone's wrongdoing. The book is not about a wrathful God seeking vengeance for every mistake. It also does not mean that if one is prosperous, it is a sign they have pleased God.

Chapters 1-2 use the techniques of narrative. The first two chapters are the Exposition and Catalyst. Chapters 3 through 41 use poetry to evoke the emotional weight of the characters. In the final chapter, the story's resolution uses narrative. In the beginning, Job directs our attention towards himself and the pain he is experiencing. By the end of the book, Job has a wider perspective.

Dialog dominates the book. Tension arises from the conflicting statements made by the characters. God and Satan discuss Job's ability to be faithful. Messengers inform Job about the death of his children and loss of his property, resulting in anguish. Job, his wife, and his friends debate whether God is punishing him for his sinfulness. Finally, God speaks up to correct the misunderstanding of Job and his friends.

Dialog shows Job's character by his insistence on his righteousness and his refusal to condemn God for his misfortune.

Job's poetry uses three types of parallelism. [2]

> 1. Synonymous parallelism states a thought in the first line, then repeats it in different words in the second line.

> 2. Antithetic parallelism reverses the statement of the first line.

> 3. Developmental parallelism uses the second line to expand upon the concept of the first line.

Job 3:11 is an example of synonymous parallelism, where the second line restates the first. Dying at birth is stated two ways.

Why did I not die at birth,

Come forth from the womb and expire? Job 3:11

Here is an example of antithetic parallelism. Note *"beginning was insignificant"* contrasts with *"end will increase greatly."*

Though your beginning was insignificant,

Yet your end will increase greatly. Job 8:7

Job 5:19 illustrates developmental parallelism. The first line uses "six troubles," and the second line increases it to "seven."

From six troubles He will deliver you,

Even in seven evil will not touch you. Job 5:19

Job cries out that he wants to present his case before God, as though it were a trial. At that time princes and kings were also judges in disputes. He demands an answer from God.

Oh that I had one to hear me!
Behold, here is my signature;
Let the Almighty answer me!
And the indictment which my adversary has written,
Surely I would carry it on my shoulder,
I would bind it to myself like a crown.
I would declare to Him the number of my steps;
Like a prince I would approach Him. Job 31:35-37

God responds out of the whirlwind, which evokes terror in the listener. He demands that Job answer Him instead and describes His omnipotence and omniscience in creating the heavens and the earth. The poet employs figurative language, likening the earth to a building with its cornerstone, foundation, and bases.

Then the Lord answered Job out of the whirlwind and said,
'... Now gird up your loins like a man,
And I will ask you, and you instruct Me!
Where were you when I laid the foundation of the earth?
Tell Me, if you have understanding,
Who set its measurements? Since you know.
Or who stretched the line on it?
On what were its bases sunk? Or who laid its cornerstone,
When the morning stars sang together
And all the sons of God shouted for joy?' Job 38:1–7

The similes and metaphors continue as the sea comes from a womb, a cloud is its garment, and bolts and doors are a barrier. This vivid imagery would have less impact if it were in prose.

Or who enclosed the sea with doors

When, bursting forth, it went out from the womb;

When I made a cloud its garment

And thick darkness its swaddling band,

And I placed boundaries on it

And set a bolt and doors,

And I said, 'Thus far you shall come, but no farther;

And here shall your proud waves stop'? Job 38:8-11

In Chapter 42, Job confesses God can do all things and is too wonderful for him to understand. Following that, the writer transitions to prose. God chastises Job's friends for their remarks concerning Him and demands a sacrifice to accept Job. God restored Job's fortunes after he prayed for his friends.

Song of Songs

The last book of wisdom is Song of Songs, also called the Song of Solomon because of its attribution to him. It contains elements of love and wisdom. In the past, the Jews considered it to be an allegory for God and Israel. The church regarded it as an allegory for its love for Jesus. The prevailing viewpoint is that the psalm centers on the concept of marital love.

Some scholars regard it as a collection of love songs, some as a drama.[3] The text suggests the need to make wise choices in marriage partners and to remain faithful in the marriage. Song of Songs follows the poetic conventions discussed above, including figurative language and poetic license.

The main characters are Solomon, a shepherd, and a Shulamite woman. Whether the speaker is Solomon or the shepherd is often unclear.

This excerpt is a man praising the beauty of the woman. The poem uses simile to describe the beloved's features. The man evokes images of goats descending from a mountain, with the old dirty wool removed, showing only clean wool. Comparing her to a dove symbolized her purity. Comparing a woman to a flock of goats or a slice of pomegranate is no longer seen as a compliment. But these were important to the culture.

How beautiful you are, my darling,
How beautiful you are!
Your eyes are like doves behind your veil;
Your hair is like a flock of goats
That have descended from Mount Gilead.
Your teeth are like a flock of newly shorn ewes
Which have come up from their washing,
All of which bear twins,
And not one among them has lost her young.
Your lips are like a scarlet thread,
And your mouth is lovely.
Your temples are like a slice of a pomegranate
Behind your veil. Song of Songs 4:1-3

In chapter five, the woman describes her beloved's hair and eyes using similes. It evokes much more imagination than stating their colors. She expresses how much she values him by comparing him to gold and myrrh. Myrrh is a fragrant oil and at the time was expensive.

His head is like gold, pure gold;
His locks are like clusters of dates
And black as a raven.
His eyes are like doves
Beside streams of water,
Bathed in milk,
And reposed in their setting.
His cheeks are like a bed of balsam,
Banks of sweet-scented herbs;

His lips are lilies

Dripping with liquid myrrh. Song of Songs 5:11-13

I hope you enjoyed reviewing the poetic techniques found in the Bible. The repetition, figurative language, and shift in point of view evoke emotions in the reader. And we also learned that with the wisdom books, taking a verse or two out of context might teach the wrong lesson.

In the next chapter, our focus will shift towards examining the literary techniques employed in the New Testament. They include narratives of Jesus in the Gospels, and a review of the role of parables in His teaching.

---

1. Fee, 243.

2. Craig G. Bartholomew, *When You Want to Yell at God: The Book of Job*, ed. Craig G. Bartholomew et. al., Transformative Word (Bellingham, WA: Lexham Press 2014), 29.

3. James E. Smith, *The Wisdom Literature and Psalms*, Old Testament Survey Series (Joplin, MO: College Press Pub. Co., 1996), 826.

Chapter Three

New Testament Gospels

The primary emphasis of this chapter will be on the New Testament accounts of Jesus' life. Our goal is to analyze the four Gospels and examine their literary choices in highlighting different aspects of Jesus' ministry. Our review will focus on the application of narrative techniques to the Gospels. We will finish by reviewing some similarities and differences in the Gospels.

The New Testament begins with the Gospels, which explore Jesus' life and ministry. They include many literary forms, such as narrative, sermons, parables, and prophecy. Chapter five will delve into prophecies.

Each Gospel tailors its narrative to a specific audience.[1] The authors included or omitted various scenes and put them in different sequences to emphasize the purpose of the book. The three synoptic Gospels (Matthew, Mark, and Luke) are similar. However, John takes a more theological perspective. The authors did not intend to conform to modern standards for histories or biographies. The narratives include Jesus' life and ministry, his sermons to the crowds, and the parables he used as a teaching technique. All authors highlighted Jesus' role in fulfilling Old Testament prophecy.

Jesus' message and the dominant cultures were in conflict.

- The Romans resorted to military violence to establish their authority, which included the expectation that subject populations would worship Roman gods and the emperors.

- The Jews expected God to send a Messiah who would be a military leader like David and free them from the Romans.

- Conversely, Jesus teaches about a spiritual kingdom and affirms His divinity as the Son of God.

About the Gospels

Each Gospel starts at a different time in its exposition. In Matthew and Luke, the anticipation of the birth of Jesus begins the narrative. At around thirty years old, His ministry begins, which is where Mark and John's accounts start. During His ministry, Jesus taught, healed, and gave the Jewish people hope. When He preached the coming of God's kingdom, the Jews expected a physical kingdom on earth. Jesus' death and resurrection promised a different liberation than the Jews expected.

- Scholars believe that John Mark, a friend of the Apostle Peter, wrote the Gospel of Mark. His audience was the persecuted church near the time of the fall of Jerusalem to the Romans. Scholars believe Matthew and Luke used Mark as a source for their books.

- Matthew's work focused on the Jewish community, emphasizing Jesus' ancestry and the fulfillment of prophecies. Scholars believe Matthew was Levi, Jesus' disciple and the tax collector.

- Luke highlighted the underprivileged individuals Jesus came to rescue. Luke was a Gentile physician and historian who made a careful record by interviewing witnesses to Jesus' ministry.

- Written years after the other Gospels, the book of John, probably by one of the twelve Apostles, was intended for Greek-speaking Christians in the first century. Knowing his readers were familiar with the other gospels, the author spent more time on Jesus' theology in his book.

Character Arcs

The Gospels are collections of narratives, also called pericopes, with Jesus as the protagonist. Unlike the typical protagonist, Jesus is not flawed. The narratives depict Him teaching and healing those who are flawed either in their spirituality or physicality, or sometimes both. Among the antagonists in the narratives are the Romans, certain figures in the Jewish leadership, King Herod, Herod's family, the Roman authorities, and Satan. His internal struggle is knowing He must die on the cross.

Many other characters have their own arcs, but there is not enough time to explore them in this book. Examining a pericope on its own is useful for determining its literary genre. But the other rules of reading it in context to understand symbols still apply.

Jesus appears to have had both internal and external struggles. Deep down, He knew that His fate was to go to Jerusalem and die on the cross. In Gethsemane's Garden, He prayed for a different outcome yet remained obedient to God's command. The external threats started with Herod the Great and continued with other Jews. They tried several times to kill Him, and He avoided Jerusalem or traveled there incognito. The Roman occupiers were always a threat to any who they suspected challenged their empire. His efforts to explain His mission and the Kingdom of God often failed. People were not ready to hear what He had to say. There were moments when He revealed His annoyance with His followers. Satan took several opportunities to tempt Jesus to betray His mission. He knew His time to teach was short, and He traveled frequently to contact as many people as possible.

Narrative Arc

In Chapter One, we presented the pyramid model for narratives. Let's see how it applies to the Gospels.

Exposition: Each Gospel had a different beginning when revealing Jesus' origins. [2]

- Matthew began with Jesus' genealogy, then told his birth story. His goal was to prove that Jesus was descended from David and fulfilled prophecy.

- Mark started with the story about John the Baptizer announcing Jesus' ministry.

- Luke recounted how he spoke to eyewitnesses of Jesus' life and ministry. The narrative began with the conception of John the Baptist, which happened prior to Mary conceiving Jesus.

- John relied on theology, emphasizing Jesus' pre-existence and divinity, before describing Jesus' early ministry.

Catalyst: Jesus' ministry began with His baptism when the Spirit descended and God spoke to Him. Subsequently, He spent forty days in the wilderness, with Satan tempting Him to go against God's will.

Rising action: Jesus moved to Capernaum, a city on an international highway. He called twelve men to be His disciples. His ministry continued for about three years, during which He taught the disciples and the populace. He went to the Jews first, then to the Gentiles. His preaching and miracles made the Jewish leaders and Romans fearful of an uprising. They did not understand the nature of His announcement of the Kingdom of God. He eluded capture until God ordained His presence in Jerusalem during Passover.

Climax: Jesus was in Galilee when He told His disciples that He would die and be resurrected. He then began His last trip to Jerusalem.

Falling action: While traveling to Jerusalem, He spoke to crowds and performed miracles. All Gospels feature the account of Jesus' arrival in Jerusalem on a colt or a donkey. Prior to Judas' betrayal in Gethsemane, He shared a Passover supper with His disciples. The Sanhedrin tried Him, then turned Him over to the Romans. Pontius Pilate crucified Him. He was buried in a tomb and the disciples went into hiding.

Resolution: The story took a surprising turn when Jesus was resurrected after three days. First, He met with the women who followed Him. Then He appeared to His disciples and other followers to explain the fulfillment of prophecies. Eventually, He ascended to heaven.

Settings

Using settings is common across all four Gospels. Many locations mentioned in the Gospels recall other events of significance in Jewish history. By examining the locations, modern readers can infer whether Jesus is in an urban or rural area and the religious background of the crowd. The Jewish or Greco-Roman locations shaped the message of the story.

Jesus was born in Bethlehem. This fulfilled a prophecy regarding the Messiah. Herod the Great attempted to murder baby Jesus, forcing his parents to flee to Egypt. When Herod died, they returned and raised Jesus in Nazareth, in a hidden valley in Zebulun. A small village, it had around four hundred residents. It provided a secure environment in which Jesus could be raised, shielded from Herod's sons.

Two locations share the name Bethany. One is near Jerusalem, the other at a site beyond the Jordan River. The latter is the site of two memorable events in the Bible (John 1:28). The first event occurred nearby when Joshua and the Jews crossed into the Promised Land (Joshua 3-4). God halted the flow of the river until the Jews crossed to the other side. The second occurred during Jesus' baptism when the heavens opened, the Spirit descended, and God declared Jesus was His Son (Matthew 3:14-17).

After being baptized, Jesus ventured into the wilderness. Steep mountains and narrow valleys characterize the harsh and dry landscape. His fast lasted forty days, during which Satan tempted Him. The ordeal is reminiscent of the forty-year journey of the Hebrews in the wilderness after their escape from Egypt. Unlike His ancestors, He remained obedient to God and rebuked Satan.

Nazareth was too isolated for Jesus to accomplish His goals. Capernaum, on the plain of Naphtali near the Sea of Galilee, provided access to an international highway. He moved there to reach a broader audience for His ministry.

In Mark, Jesus spent much time near the Sea of Galilee and visiting Gentile cities. He attempted to avoid the Jewish leadership because He knew they would perceive His message as a threat. In contrast, Jerusalem was the primary setting for much of the action in John.

Mount Arbel, near the Sea of Galilee, was an important site. It's likely that this is the place where Jesus delivered the Sermon on the Mount. On the seashore, fisherfolk packed fish in salt to preserve them for sale. Jesus' comment about a city on a hill giving off light may have been the Greek city Hippos, across the sea, which was lit at night and visible for miles. After His resurrection, He gathered with the disciples on a mountain near Galilee. The existence of an international highway and Greek cities across the sea would have made His command to go into the world more meaningful.

Dialog and sermons

Jesus' dialog merits special attention because it offers valuable insight into His thoughts and interactions. Frequently called rabbi (meaning teacher), He delivered sermons to crowds, which included parables. He explained the parables to the twelve disciples in private. Besides Jewish men, Jesus had conversations with both Gentiles and women. Jewish law at the time forbade men to interact with Gentiles and women because they were seen as ritually unclean. He didn't hesitate to correct the Scribes and Pharisees when they challenged Him. Several times, He chastised Satan or his demons. During His trials, He declared His divinity to the Sanhedrin and Pontius Pilot.

Parables

Jesus used parables as a teaching tool during His ministry. Parables are folk literature, part of the culture's oral traditions. People sometimes refer to shorter ones as metaphors or similes.

Real-life encounters formed the basis for parables, ensuring solid teachings. For instance, the characters plant fields, tend sheep, and attend weddings, just like Jesus' contemporaries. The plots are simple, involving few or no changes of setting. Often there is a conflict between the characters. This prompts the listener to choose between the two characters. Repetition emphasized the point of the story.

Ryken's book outlines the following steps for interpreting parables. [3]

    1. Examine the story to determine what the listener understands first. For example, in the parable of the Good Seed, a man scatters seeds that land on four types of soil.

2. Interpret the symbols used in the story. Seed symbolizes the Word. The type of soil symbolizes the person's receptiveness. Whether the seed bears fruit depends on the recipient's character.

3. Look for a theme. The paragraphs before and after the parable may reveal the theme. For example, in the parable of the woman and the lost coins, there are additional paragraphs that portray a person losing and then locating something. Or it may be Jesus' response to a question from those gathered, such as the man who asked, "Who is my neighbor?"

4. Find the real-world application of the moral lesson. The Samaritan was a neighbor to the Jew, despite their longstanding animosities.

Archetypes, which are universal characters or patterns, are a characteristic of parables. Included in archetypes are roles such as master and servant, something lost and then found, and two sons, one of whom is obedient and the other not.

Parables can have multiple interpretations. The Prodigal son has at least three, one for each of the main characters. The story of The Sower with four soil types has more than one interpretation. At the disciples' request, Jesus explained the meanings when they were away from the crowds. He used these secular stories for a religious purpose.

Jesus employed suspense to engage the listener, often delivering a surprise ending. He sometimes used foils, such as wise and foolish virgins, or a rich man and a poor one. The listener chooses one of the characters to support, which Jesus used to teach a moral lesson. The characters, except for the parable about Lazarus, do not have names. However, people refer to them as the Good Samaritan, the Wise Virgins, and the owner of the vineyard.

Matthew recounts that when Jesus was in the Temple, He told parables about God sending His prophets and then His Son, and they were mistreated or killed. The Jewish leaders in the Temple at the time suspected He spoke about them. One parable was about two sons, one obedient and the other disobedient (Matthew 21:28-32). He recounted a story about a vineyard owner who entrusted the land to his tenants while he was away. But the tenants beat or killed the landowner's messengers (Matthew 21:33-44). Another parable told of a marriage feast when the king invited people to the feast. They declined, and mistreated or killed the king's servants. The king invited others to be his guests instead (Matthew 22:1-14). The parable of the wise and foolish virgins highlighted the significance of being prepared for the coming kingdom (Matthew 25:1-13).

———◦———

Let's examine the Gospels one by one, beginning with Mark, the briefest of the four Gospels. We will pay attention to parables, settings, and dialog.

Mark

A technique identified in Mark's Gospel is called a Markan sandwich. It happens when the author begins story A, then interrupts it with story B, with different characters and plot. At the conclusion of story B, the author resumes story A. Story B reinforces the teaching of story A. An example is Mark 5:22-43, which begins with Jairus asking Jesus to heal his daughter (story A). On His way to Jairus' house (Mark 5:22-24), Jesus encountered a woman who had been hemorrhaging for years (Mark 5:25-34). By touching His garment, she experienced healing (story B). The story of Jairus' daughter (story A) continues in verse 35 when Jesus resumes His journey to the house to heal the daughter. This lesson underscores the importance of faith for those seeking healing.

Mark uses the adverb "immediately" over thirty times. In the first chapter, John baptizes his cousin Jesus, who then selects His disciples in Galilee. Jesus wastes no time casting out demons, speaking to crowds, and healing the sick.

Jesus refers to Himself as the "Son of Man," based on Daniel 7:13. In the second chapter, Mark uses dialog between Jesus and the Pharisees to reveal conflict regarding healing on the Sabbath.

Mark's narrative depicts Jesus and His disciples constantly moving to new locations, but most of the settings are in Galilee and non-Jewish cities. Jesus went to the Gerasene region on the east shore of the Sea of Galilee. There He encountered a man possessed by demons in a cemetery. He banished the demons, who then possessed a nearby herd of pigs (Mark 5:19-20). This suggests Gentile culture dominated the region. On His second visit, a large crowd gathered to hear Him speak (Mark 7:31-8:13). Jesus performed His second miracle involving feeding, this time four thousand. Although terrified of His actions the first time, people flocked to hear Him the second time.

After Jesus had performed the miracles of feeding the crowds twice, the disciples discuss they had no bread. Jesus expresses His frustration with their lack of understanding.

[The disciples] began to discuss with one another the fact that they had no bread.

And Jesus, aware of this, said to them, 'Why do you discuss the fact that you have no bread? Do you not yet see or understand? Do you have a hardened heart?

'Having eyes, do you not see? And having ears, do you not hear? And do you

not remember, when I broke the five loaves for the five thousand, how many baskets full of broken pieces you picked up?' They said to Him, 'Twelve.'

'When I broke the seven for the four thousand, how many large baskets full of broken pieces did you pick up?' And they said to Him, 'Seven.'

And He was saying to them, 'Do you not yet understand?' Mark 8:16-21

Matthew

Now we will turn to Matthew, the first book of the New Testament, likely written after the destruction of the Jewish Temple. The narrative emphasizes Jesus' genealogy through Solomon and David, and beyond to Abraham. Matthew describes the angel's appearance to Joseph and references the Old Testament prophecies about the Messiah. Magi, who brought gifts for a king, visited Jesus and His parents after He was born. This book includes the escape to Egypt to fulfill prophecy as well.

Matthew referred to Jesus as Rabbi or Teacher over sixteen times. Jesus referred to himself as the "Son of Man" twenty-eight times. He was called the Messiah four times. Matthew used the phrase "kingdom of heaven," but Mark, Luke, and John used the phrase "kingdom of God." Matthew highlights Jesus' ministry in Galilee. He also went to Gentile locations in Tyre, Sidon, Bethsaida, and Caesarea Philippi.

Matthew distinguishes the beginning and end of Jesus' sermons to the crowds from his interactions with individuals. For example, let's look at the Sermon on the Mount starting in Matthew 5. Jesus started with *"He opened His mouth and began to teach them, saying, ..."* The sermon continues through Chapter 7, and ends with, *"When Jesus had finished these words, the crowds were amazed at His teaching...."*

Matthew showed Jesus' humanity when he included dialog in which Jesus expressed frustration with His disciples after they failed to cast out a demon.

And Jesus answered and said, "You unbelieving and perverted generation, how long shall I be with you? How long shall I put up with you? Bring him here to Me." Matthew 17:17

In Tyre and Sidon, where pagan worship was still prevalent, Jesus displayed His power over pagan gods through a miracle of healing. A Syrophoenician woman who was not a Jew asked Jesus to heal her daughter.

And He [Jesus] answered and said, "It is not good to take the children's bread and throw it to the dogs."

But she said, "Yes, Lord; but even the dogs feed on the crumbs which fall from their masters' table."

Then Jesus said to her, "O woman, your faith is great; it shall be done for you as you wish." And her daughter was healed at once. Matthew 15:24–28

This setting references the story of Jezebel, the Sidonian wife of King Ahab. She worshipped Baal and practiced sorcery. She was responsible for the death of many Jewish prophets, and dogs eventually killed her (1 Kings 16).

Luke

Now we will review the Gospel written by Luke, a Gentile physician, and historian. He used Mark's narrative as a basis for his book but improved the Greek and changed the order of some pericopes. He also interviewed eyewitnesses to Jesus' life.

Luke has more discourse than action. He wrote about the poor and disadvantaged people to whom Jesus ministered. In Luke's accounts, he portrayed Jesus ministering to a diverse range of individuals, including Gentiles and women. Mary's Magnificat praises God for giving good things to the poor while scattering the proud and unseating the rich from their thrones.

As a historian, Luke began with the story of John the Baptizer's conception, linking him to Elijah. He recounted the angel appearing to Mary, John's birth, and Jesus' birth. In his version, shepherds in the fields near Bethlehem came to worship the newborn. This book also includes the story of Jesus at the Temple at age twelve and how He impressed the teachers with His wisdom.

Jesus' genealogy is in Luke 3, but it differs from Matthew. Luke followed the genealogy back to Adam through Nathan and David, while Matthew followed it through Solomon.

Luke compared Jesus' ministry to that of previous Jewish prophets sent by God but rejected by His people. This example is from Luke 4:18-21. The setting is the synagogue in Nazareth. Jesus reads from Isaiah 58 and 61, which declare healing for the sick and freedom for the prisoners. Then, He announces the prophecy fulfilled on that day and place. When He recounts God sent prophets Elijah and Elisha outside of Israel, they attempted to kill Him.

And He said, "Truly I say to you, no prophet is welcome in his hometown.

"But I say to you in truth, there were many widows in Israel in the days of Elijah, when the sky was shut up for three years and six months, when a great famine came over all the land;

and yet Elijah was sent to none of them, but only to Zarephath, in the land of Sidon, to a woman who was a widow.

"And there were many lepers in Israel in the time of Elisha the prophet; and none of them was cleansed, but only Naaman the Syrian."

And all the people in the synagogue were filled with rage as they heard these things;

and they got up and drove Him out of the city, and led Him to the brow of the hill on which their city had been built, in order to throw Him down the cliff.

But passing through their midst, He went His way. Luke 4:24-30.

Bethany and Bethpage, two villages near Jerusalem, were important settings for Luke. Jesus' friends Mary, Martha, and Lazarus lived in Bethany. Luke 10:38-42 details Martha's grievance with Mary for choosing to listen to Jesus instead of helping with the meal. Jesus defends Mary's decision as being the better one.

Prior to His last journey to Jerusalem, Jesus stayed in Bethany while the disciples went to Bethpage to retrieve a donkey for Him. Centuries earlier, Solomon rode King David's donkey from Bethpage to Gihon Spring in Jerusalem to be coronated King of Israel (1 Kings 1:32-40). Jesus entered Jerusalem on the donkey and followed the same route as Solomon to symbolize His claim to be the King of the Jews.

John

The fourth Gospel, the book of John, takes a different approach to telling Jesus' story. From the beginning, he emphasized Jesus was divine. John focused on dialog and the complexity of Jesus' statements. This Gospel also contains narratives not found in the Synoptic Gospels. Examples of this are the wedding at Cana when He changed water into wine; the conversation with Nicodemus about needing to be born again; and the conversation with the Samaritan woman about living water. This is the only one to use the phrase "Lamb of God."

John emphasized Jesus' divinity when His friend Lazarus died in Bethany. Jesus traveled to the village where Martha confronted Him about not arriving sooner to heal her brother. Their dialog is recorded below.

Jesus said to her, "Your brother will rise again."

Martha said to Him, "I know that he will rise again in the resurrection on the last day."

Jesus said to her, "I am the resurrection and the life; he who believes in Me will live even if he dies, and everyone who lives and believes in Me will never die. Do you believe this?"

She said to Him, "Yes, Lord; I have believed that You are the Christ, the Son of God, even He who comes into the world." John 11:23-27

Soon after, He brought Lazarus back to life.

Jesus used metaphor as a teaching technique. John included a series of "I AM ..." statements made by Jesus, which were rich with symbolism.

- *"I AM the bread of life"*

- *"I AM the light of the world"*

- *"I AM the door"*

- *"I AM the good shepherd"*

- *"I AM the resurrection and the life"*

- *"I AM the way, the truth, and the life"*

- *"I AM the true vine"*

It reminded the Jews of God, who referred to Himself as "I AM" in Exodus 3:14.

John emphasized that Jesus' conversations often had a physical and a spiritual meaning. Here, the disciples urged Jesus to eat physical food, while Jesus assured them He had spiritual food.

Meanwhile the disciples were urging Him, saying, 'Rabbi, eat.'
But He said to them, 'I have food to eat that you do not know about.'
So the disciples were saying to one another, 'No one brought Him anything

to eat, did he?'

Jesus said to them, 'My food is to do the will of Him who sent Me and to accomplish His work.' John 4:31-34

Jesus and Nicodemus had a conversation about being born again, providing another example. Nicodemus thought Jesus meant physical rebirth, but Jesus meant spiritual rebirth.

... [Nicodemus] said to Him, "Rabbi, we know that You have come from God as a teacher; for no one can do these signs that You do unless God is with him."

Jesus answered and said to him, "Truly, truly, I say to you, unless one is born again he cannot see the kingdom of God."

Nicodemus said to Him, "How can a man be born when he is old? He cannot enter a second time into his mother's womb and be born, can he?"

Jesus answered, "Truly, truly, I say to you, unless one is born of water and the Spirit he cannot enter into the kingdom of God.

"That which is born of the flesh is flesh, and that which is born of the Spirit is spirit.

"Do not be amazed that I said to you, 'You must be born again.'

"The wind blows where it wishes and you hear the sound of it, but do not know where it comes from and where it is going; so is everyone who is born of the Spirit." John 3:2-8

John conflates Passover and Yom Kippur in recounting Jesus' death. On Yom Kippur, the Day of Atonement, Jews transfer their sins to a goat, which is driven into the wilderness to die. Passover is a festival of celebration remembering the freedom from slavery in Egypt. John connects Jesus' death to the Day of Preparation for Passover, which involves sacrificing lambs for the celebration. Reinforcing the symbolism of Jesus as the sacrificial Lamb, this Gospel added meaning by proclaiming Jesus to be the Lamb who takes away the sins of the world.

———— ❖ ————

The primary aim of this chapter was to examine and discuss the literary techniques that are found in the New Testament Gospels. The Gospel writers took different approaches in recounting the life of Jesus, with each writer adopting their own distinctive style. Our study delved into the role of settings and dialogs in the storytelling process, aiming to understand how authors use them. Next, we examined the similarities and differences in their narratives. Parables played a crucial role in Jesus' teachings, acting as a fundamental building block in the delivery of His message. We examined ways to derive the meaning from the parables.

Our next chapter will look at the Book of Acts as an example of history, and the letters as a literary genre. Acts gives us insight into the daily lives of members of the fledgling church, and its spread through the Holy Spirit. Letters communicate some of the important issues of the time.

---

1. Judy Yates Siker and Patricia Lynn Miller, *Who Is Jesus? What a Difference a Lens Makes*, Horizons Presbyterian Women, Inc., (Presbyterian Church USA, 2016).

2. Siker, *Who is Jesus?*

3. Ryken, 151-152.

Chapter Four

Acts and Letters

T his chapter will focus on the early Christian church. We will explore the Book of Acts, which covers the time when most of the letters were written. Then we will review the literary techniques used by the authors of the letters and epistles.

The Book of Acts includes several literary genres. The story focuses on the actions of Peter, Paul, and others during the early days of the church. The author's writing style adheres to the popular historical format of the time. This covers how the Holy Spirit influenced the spread from Jesus' resurrection to Paul's later imprisonment in Rome. Included are several apologetic sermons which the apostles delivered to defend their faith against the Jews and Gentiles who opposed them.

The social conditions of the era shaped the disciples' actions and teachings. Roman cities benefitting from trade routes were wealthy, while conquered regions such as Palestine were poor. People conquered by the mighty Roman military became slaves. Their labor built the empire's buildings and roads and provided food for Rome. Roman armies controlled the provinces. Poverty, disease, and famine were common and affected the Jerusalem church.

Several obstacles hinder our understanding of the narrative. Two thousand years separate us from the culture and traditions of the time. The authors spoke Aramaic and Hellenistic Greek. Scholars sometimes differ on the correct translation of the words. There are references to conversations or experiences about which we lack information. With the letters, we read only one side of the conversation.

According to Fee, when reading these narratives and letters, it's important for the modern reader to distinguish between "...what is cultural and therefore belongs to the first century alone and what transcends culture and is thus a Word for all seasons."[1]

About Acts

What do we know about the author of Acts? Luke is a Gentile, a physician, and a historian. He also wrote the Gospel of Luke. His primary language and culture are Greek, so he writes in the tradition of Greek historians. Luke conducted interviews with those involved, and even traveled with Paul in his later years. He records Divine activity in the spread of the early church. Luke's target audience was the Greek speaking Christians, most of whom were Gentile converts.

Structure of Acts

Luke groups events into six distinct phases in the Church's development. He makes note of the presence of the Holy Spirit at each stage. Notice the dominance of dialog in the narratives.

Stage one Acts 1:1-6:7: The early Jerusalem church continued Jewish customs.

Characters:

- Jesus, the apostles, and the disciples

- Holy Spirit

- Sanhedrin

- Aramaic speaking Jews

Location:
- Jerusalem

This stage begins with Jesus' ascension to heaven, and the disciples' vigil in Jerusalem until Pentecost. The Holy Spirit descended on them, and they spoke in tongues. Thousands of Jews began to follow Jesus. However, the Jewish leaders considered it blasphemy and arrested many of the followers. Peter was prominent in the narratives which occurred in Jerusalem. Notice the character development in which Peter starts as a fisherman hiding in an upper room but becomes a leader and gains recognition as an orator who heals the sick and converts thousands.

Stage two Acts 6:8-9:31: The church broadens to include Greek-speaking Jews.

Characters:
- Holy Spirit

- Stephen

- Peter, John, Philip

- Saul/Paul

- Greek-speaking Jews

Location:
- Jerusalem

- Samaria

- Damascus

Hellenistic Jews arrive from regions beyond Jerusalem, such as Samaria. Hellenist Jews of Synagogue of the Freedmen martyr Stephen. When Philip travels to Samaria, he converts and baptizes many people. But it is not until Peter and John lay hands on them that they receive the Holy Spirit.

Saul, a Hellenist Jew later known as Paul, becomes a zealous persecutor of the Christ followers. This stage records his conversion when he encounters Jesus on the road to Damascus. From then on, his mission is to be an apostle and spread the good news of Christ.

Stage three Acts 9:32-12:24: Baptism of Gentiles; founding of the church in Antioch.

Characters:

- Holy Spirit

- Peter

- Cornelius, a Roman centurion

- Barnabas, Saul/Paul

Location:

- Jerusalem

- Caesarea, Joppa, and Lydda

- Antioch

Luke records the expansion of the church to Antioch and acceptance of Gentiles as converts. Peter's character develops as he travels to Caesarea, Joppa, and Lydda. Peter experiences a vision about clean and unclean animals which leads to him baptizing a Roman Centurion. He is persuasive in convincing the leaders in Jerusalem to include Gentiles as Christ followers. Barnabas and Saul spend a year in Antioch to nurture the church.

Stage four Acts 12:25-16:5: Missionary journey beyond Palestine and Judea; Jerusalem's council clarifies rules for Gentile converts.

Characters:

- Holy Spirit

- Paul, Barnabas, John Mark

- Peter, James, Jerusalem Council

Location:

- Jerusalem, Antioch

- Perga

- Pisidian Antioch, Lystra, etc.

The Holy Spirit sends Paul and Barnabas to Cyprus. They continue to Perga, then to Pisidian Antioch, where they preach to Jews and God fearers. Tension increases as Jewish opposition forces Paul and Barnabas to flee to Iconium and other cities. In Lystra, a mob stoned Paul after he and Barnabas were mistaken for Greek gods. He and Barnabas returned to Antioch.

Jews journey from Judea to Antioch to instruct Gentile converts to follow Jewish laws. Paul and Barnabas object, and travel to Jerusalem to appeal to the council of apostles and elders. Peter supported Paul and Barnabas. Based on the council's decision, James wrote a letter to churches in Antioch, Syria, and Cicilia attributing the decision to the Holy Spirit.

"For it seemed good to the Holy Spirit and to us to lay upon you no greater

burden than these essentials: that you abstain from things sacrificed to idols and from blood and from things strangled and from fornication; if you keep yourselves free from such things, you will do well. Farewell." Acts 15:28-29

The Gentiles would not be required to undergo circumcision or adhere to the dietary laws of the Jews.

Stage five Acts16:6-19:20: Expansion in Europe, conflict with Jews.

Characters:

- Holy Spirit

- Paul and Silas

- Luke joins Paul briefly

Locations:

- Antioch

- Macedonia

Tensions rise and conflict intensifies. While Paul and Silas journeyed to Macedonia, Barnabas traveled with John Mark. Paul's travels and sermons are the focus of Luke's writings. The Holy Spirit directed Paul, guiding him to stay away from Asia.

In Acts 16:13, when Paul was in Phillipi, the narrator shifts from "they" to "we." Scholars believe Luke joined Paul during his journey. By chapter seventeen, the narrator resumes the use of "they." Paul and Silas faced imprisonment and beatings in several cities. They completed two separate missionary trips in Europe. Acts 18:2 includes references to the Roman Jews forced to leave Rome by Emperor Claudius.

Stage six Acts19:21-28:30: Paul goes to Europe and Asia, and journeys to Rome.

Characters:

- Holy Spirit

- Felix, Agrippa, Lysias, Festus

- Paul, Luke

- Captain and sailors

Locations:
- Jerusalem

- Caesarea-Philippi

- Malta

- Rome

This was the last stage that Luke recorded. Paul traveled to Macedonia and Greece. In Acts 20:6, Luke again joins Paul. The Holy Spirit warned Paul not to return to Jerusalem, but he traveled there intending to help the impoverished Jerusalem church. Jews from other cities stirred up a mob against him. The Roman soldiers intervened to stop the mob, and then they arrested Paul. Guided by the Holy Spirit, he persistently proclaimed his innocence. He stayed in prison for years before exercising his right as a Roman citizen to appeal to the emperor. After an arduous trip to Rome during which he was shipwrecked, he remained under arrest, always accompanied by a Roman guard. During the next two years, he wrote letters to the churches and to his friends. There, the record from Luke s tops.

Next, we will look at some letters and epistles written by Paul and other Christ followers during this time.

Letters and Epistles

What is the difference between letters and epistles? Authors designed epistles, like 2 Peter and 1 John, for public consumption. Despite being shared with others, letters retain their personal nature. Letters address individual needs and are not intended to be theological tracts. Some letters diverge from the standard format, being written as tracts or sermons. For example, Hebrews is part tract and part letter. The letter from James reads like a collection of sermons. For our purposes, the term letters will include all books starting with "Letter to ...."

The letters are the largest component of the New Testament. They are all from the first century. They are important because not only did the recipients read the letters, but they also passed them from one church to another and read them aloud, combining public and private communication.

Scholars consider the letters an occasional document. The writer's text is a response to a query from the reader, or a comment made by another individual about the topic. However, the authors of James, Philemon, and Romans were the originators, setting them apart. They were specific to the needs of the recipients.

The writers composed the letters intending to fulfill several objectives, which included giving instruction, correcting behavior, responding to questions, offering encouragement, and clarifying beliefs. In some cases scholars disagree as to the identity of the author of the letter. What is important is that the ideas expressed in the letter are consistent with the messages of the Gospels and the other letters.

Paul authored most of the letters. Scholars categorize Paul's letters into various groups. His Pastoral epistles dealing with church leadership issues are 1 and 2 Timothy and Titus. Others attributed to Paul are Romans, 1 and 2 Corinthians, Galatians, Philippians, 1 Thessalonians, and Philemon. Those attributed to Paul but thought by some to be by other authors are Ephesians, Colossians, and 2 Thessalonians. Ephesians, Colossians, Philippians, and Philemon were probably written when Paul was in prison i n Rome.

Scholars now believe Apollos wrote Hebrews. Apollos, a Jewish teacher from Egypt who met Paul in Ephesus, was mentioned by Paul in several letters. The letter to the Hebrews aimed at Jewish converts to Christianity who were contemplating returning to their Jewish roots.

In addition, James (a half-brother of Jesus and leader of the Jerusalem church), the Apostle Peter, the Apostle John (son of Zebedee), and Jude (a brother of James), wrote letters to the dispersed churches.

The two letters by Peter went to five districts in Asia Minor. The three letters by John also went to Asia minor. It is probable that John wrote his letters last, dating back to the 90s CE. James wrote to Jews who became Christians. Jude and 2 Peter might have been written around the same time, as they both address the same issue of false teaching.

Structure and interpretation

Letters possess a distinctive structure that sets them apart as a genre of literature. The letters followed a predictable pattern widely used at the time: [2]

    1. The salutation gave the names of the sender and his expected reader(s).

2. A greeting.

3. A prayer of thanksgiving.

4. The body, in which the writer explained the purpose of the letter.

5. The closing, including greetings to others at the church and a benediction.

Here are some suggestions for reading these letters.[3] Read the entire letter at one time before trying to analyze specific verses. Then read by paragraph and outline the issues in each. Understanding the letter's purpose and the recommended actions may require multiple readings. For example, Paul writes in arguments and sometimes circles around to close his argument. A commentary will provide historical and cultural information as well as discuss differing translations and interpretations. The Book of Acts provides background as well.

Characters and setting

When reading the letters, it's important to focus on certain details. The first is to make a note of the people referenced in the document. Are they rural or urban, rich or poor, Jew or Gentile, young or old, male or female, and slave or free? This may make a difference in their role in the local church and how the author approaches them. It's important to consider the author's attitude toward their audience. Is he fatherly, encouraging, scolding, exasperated, fond?

The setting is likewise important. Is it Jewish or Gentile? Is it on a trade route or more remote? Is the city wealthy or struggling to recover from some disaster? What are the religious artifacts and shrines? Did the setting have any notable features, such as a specific crop or manufactured item? You will need to check historical references to find out this information.

Literary techniques

Letters might include allusions to poetry, proverbs, and storytelling. Paul used rhetorical techniques like those used by Greek scholars when delivering his messages. Other literary devices are techniques mentioned in the chapter on poetry. The following are some illustrations of the different techniques incorporated in the letters.

Here is an example of a proverb. It's a single line imparting a wise lesson.

Do not be deceived: 'Bad company corrupts good morals.' 1 Corinthians 15:33

Next is an example of poetry. Notice the rhythm as each line builds on the previous one.

By common confession, great is the mystery of godliness:
He who was revealed in the flesh,
Was vindicated in the Spirit,
Seen by angels,
Proclaimed among the nations,
Believed on in the world,
Taken up in glory. 1 Timothy 3:16

Paul is known for asking rhetorical questions. That is, he inquires about something he already knows.

What then shall we say to these things? If God is for us, who is against us? Romans 8:31

Remember apostrophe? It assigns human-like qualities to inanimate objects through speech. Here he speaks to death as if it were a person and he expects a reply.

O death, where is your victory? O death, where is your sting? 1 Corinthians 15:55

Next is an example of a paradox - a situation with two contradictory statements that can't be true at the same time.

Therefore I am well content with weaknesses, with insults, with distresses, with persecutions, with difficulties, for Christ's sake; for when I am weak, then I am strong. 2 Corinthians 12:10

Below is an example of a rhetorical argument from Paul's letter to the Romans. Notice the repeated use of "for" to make his statements. He uses "so then" and "but" to qualify or negate the previous assertion. The word "therefore" points to the conclusion of his argument. To follow his argument, the reader must pay close attention.

For I know that nothing good dwells in me, that is, in my flesh;

for the willing is present in me,

but the doing of the good is not.

For the good that I want, I do not do,

but I practice the very evil that I do not want.

But if I am doing the very thing I do not want, I am no longer the one doing it, but sin which dwells in me.

I find then the principle that evil is present in me, the one who wants to do good.

For I joyfully concur with the law of God in the inner man,

but I see a different law in the members of my body, waging war against the law of my mind and making me a prisoner of the law of sin which is in my members...

Who will set me free from the body of this death? Thanks be to God through Jesus Christ our Lord!

So then, on the one hand I myself with my mind am serving the law of God,

but on the other, with my flesh the law of sin.

Therefore there is now no condemnation for those who are in Christ Jesus. Romans 7:18-8:1

Letters in Revelation

In addition to the letters already noted, John also wrote the book of Revelation, which begins with letters to seven churches. By the end of the first century CE, John lived in exile on the island of Patmos. Christians in cities dominated by the Romans suffered from severe persecution. They knew about Jesus' promise to return and bring an end to their suffering. The letters offered them hope. We will explore the prophetic aspects of Revelation in the next chapter. The cities are Ephesus, Smyrna, Pergamum, Thyatira, Sardis, Philadelphia, and Laodicea.

In each of the seven cities, the populace erected shrines to the Roman gods, such as Apollo, Athena, Dionysus, and Zeus. They also worshipped emperors Augustus or Domitian. Worshiping them was mandatory for the people of each city. Failure to do so meant ostracism, arrest, torture, even death. To conduct business, residents were required to be members of a trade guild and worship the patron deities. The Christians believed Jesus was Lord, and the emperor was not, so they were frequent targets of persecution.

The letters were divine messages. God provided the information to Jesus, who directed the Spirit. The Spirit directed the angels who appeared to John through dreams or visions. John wrote the letters and sent them to the churches. John labels himself as the scribe, while crediting Jesus and God for the message. He wrote in the Spirit, providing authority to the letters.

Remember that an important symbol for the Jews is the number seven. The seven golden lampstands symbolized the churches. The seven stars are the angels of the seven churches.

Each letter consists of seven sections.

    1. Addresses the intended recipient.

2. Attributes the source of the message.

3. Acknowledges the strengths of the church.

4. Points out the weaknesses of the church.

5. Commands them to correct their weaknesses.

6. Calls on them to listen to the Spirit.

7. Challenges them to overcome their limitations.

The letters employed figurative language, such as metaphors and similes. Here is an example of a simile in the letter to the Church of Thyatira.

The Son of God, who has eyes like a flame of fire, and His feet are like burnished bronze .... Revelation 2:18

In the letter to Sardis, Jesus is not intending to steal anything, but He compares His coming to the stealth and timing of a thief. Their spiritual sleep makes a way for sin to infiltrate their church.

Therefore if you do not wake up, I will come like a thief, and you will not know at what hour I will come to you. Revelation 3:3

There are a few metaphors within the letters.

As for the mystery of the seven stars which you saw in My right hand, and the seven golden lampstands: the seven stars are the angels of the seven churches, and the seven lampstands are the seven churches. Revelation 1:20

In the metaphor below, the woman's real name is not Jezebel. This woman is being compared to the wife of King Ahab, who worshipped Baal and who practiced sorcery. Using this name accuses the woman of worshipping pagan gods and sorcery as well.

But I have this against you, that you tolerate the woman Jezebel, who calls herself a prophetess, and she teaches and leads My bond-servants astray so that they commit acts of immorality and eat things sacrificed to idols. Revelation 2:20

Here is a well-known verse showing figurative language. Jesus is not literally knocking on the door of our house or place of business. But He is trying to get our attention so we will be receptive to His message.

Behold, I stand at the door and knock; if anyone hears My voice and opens the door, I will come in to him and will dine with him, and he with Me. Revelation 3:20

Each letter has a warning and a promise. They repeat the phrase attributed to Jesus:

He who has an ear, let him hear what the Spirit says to the churches. Revelation 2:7, 11, 17, 29, 3:6, 13, 22

In closing, Jesus encouraged them to overcome the temptation to sin, assuring them of their reward. The reward was different for each church.

He who overcomes.... Revelation 2:7, 11, 17, 26-28, 3:5, 12, 21

By studying the Book of Acts and first-century letters in this chapter, we gained insights into the church's early growth. By reading Acts and the letters, we get a sense of their daily life. We learned more about the writers, with a focus on Paul. We also identified some obstacles to understanding the contents. To gain a clearer understanding of historical details that may not be obvious, I suggest reading a commentary when analyzing Acts and the letters.

Luke wrote the Book of Acts to record the history of the spread of the church and the influence of the Holy Spirit. It consists of narrative and apologetic sermons. Religious leaders used the standard format for letters of that time to communicate with the early Christians. We examined the differences between letters and epistles and identified the authors of the letters. The key concept is that the authors of the letters did not intend to create a comprehensive theology but to address individual points of misunderstanding or clarify teaching.

Our final chapter will look at the role of prophets in both the Old and New Testaments. Our exploration will focus on texts that are divinely inspired and contain prophetic and apocalyptic elements.

---

1. Fee, 71.

2. Ryken, 155.

3. Fee, 59-60.

Chapter Five

Visionary Literature

T he topic of this chapter is visionary literature, which includes prophetic and apocalyptic writing. Let's explore the writings of the main prophets from the Old and New Testaments and discuss their prophecies. Prophecies are also called oracles. An apocalyptic prophecy stands out as a distinct category with notable variations.

Visionary literature compels individuals to use their imaginations and visualize unfamiliar scenes and characters. It encourages them to consider alternate realities. It relies on symbols and figurative language to stimulate the senses and grab their attention. Scholars debate why God gives prophecy in symbols. Perhaps He does not want us to know too much about the future. When the prophet makes predictions about things that are happening soon, he or she provides more specific details. Events that are far away in time are often less specific.[1]

Prophets receive God's or angels' messages during visions or dreams. The heavenly being starts a dialog with the prophet, who listens to the message and asks questions for clarification. The prophet then goes to the rulers or among the people and repeats what they learned. Sometimes, prophets received instructions to write and seal warnings of an apocalyptic nature that would be revealed later.

Both the Old and New Testaments contain visionary literature. The books frequently arrange oracles in a dialogue, although they may also present them as a series of messages. The practice of placing individual oracles in succession can make it challenging to tell them apart. Oracles use poetic conventions, such as figurative language, simile, and metaphor.

The elements of visionary literature set it apart from narratives. Brief scenes appear and disappear like in a dream. An oracle lacks a plot and character development. Dialog tends to be brief.

There are many prophets in the Bible. True prophets represent God and give Him credit for the message. False prophets worship the pagan deities such as Baal or the Greek and Roman gods. People believed demons inspired or possessed the pagan prophets.

This is what Peter wrote when he warned the church about false prophets.

... no prophecy of Scripture is a matter of one's own interpretation, for no prophecy was ever made by an act of human will, but men moved by the Holy Spirit spoke from God. 2 Peter 1:20-21

The role of the prophet was a heavy burden. It was the prophets' duty, as commanded by God, to deliver His message to rulers. Sometimes, the rulers took offense and tortured or executed the prophet. These are God's instructions to Ezekiel.

'Son of man, I have appointed you a watchman to the house of Israel; whenever you hear a word from My mouth, warn them from Me.' Ezekiel 3:17

'But if the watchman sees the sword coming and does not blow the trumpet and the people are not warned, and a sword comes and takes a person from them, he is taken away in his iniquity; but his blood I will require from the watchman's hand.' Ezekiel 33:6.

Historical context

During the time of the Old Testament prophets, empires were frequently at war, resulting in shifts in national boundaries. Among them were the Assyrians, the Babylonians, the Egyptians, the Persians, and the Medes. Rulers forced entire populations to relocate. The rulers imposed their religious beliefs on the conquered peoples. The Jews turned from God and adopted pagan practices, leading to the desecration of the Temple. God sent His prophets to warn the Jews of catastrophe if they did not repent.

The Old Testament includes prophetic books written between 760 and 460 BCE. The Old Testament prophets delivered oracles focused on the near future of Israel and Judah. However, some prophets had visions of the end times and Day of Judgment.

Jewish religious leaders in the fifth century BCE believed that something quenched the Spirit, resulting in the end of prophecy. Books from that period until Jesus' birth have a lesser status compared to those in the Old and New Testaments. Meanwhile, the Jews had a deep longing for a Messiah to appear and bring back their kingdom.

Exercising caution is essential when interpreting current events in relation to biblical prophecy. References are to historical and cultural events that took place over two thousand years in the past. Scholars believe less than one percent of Old Testament prophecy is still unfulfilled.[2]

This list includes some of the better-known Old Testament prophets.

- Joseph (Genesis)

- Moses (Exodus-Deuteronomy)

- Samuel (1 & 2 Samuel)

- Nathan (2 Samuel)

- Elijah (1 & 2 Kings)

• Elisha (2 Kings)

The distinction between major and minor in the sixteen books of prophecy is determined by the length of the writing, not the importance. A single scroll contains the writings of multiple minor prophets.

Major prophets : Isaiah, Jeremiah, Ezekiel, Daniel.

Minor prophets: Hosea, Joel, Amos, Obadiah, Jonah, Micah, Nahum, Habakkuk, Zephaniah, Haggai, Zechariah, and Malachi.

Typically, the prophets were men, but the Bible mentions a few women. They are Miriam (Exodus 15:20), Deborah (Judges 4:4), Huldah (2 Kings 22:14), Noadiah (Nehemiah 6:14), un-named prophetess (Isaiah 8:3), and Anna (Luke 2:36).

Jezebel was a false prophetess (Revelation 2:20). The first-century church acknowledged women as prophets and allowed them to take part in prophesying (1 Corinthians 11:5, Acts 21:9).

Signs and warnings

Prophets warned the people to look for signs. Frequent signs are the sun, moon, and stars being dark or turning blood-red. In several books, God warned the Jews of the destruction of Israel in 722 BCE by Assyria and of Judah in 587 BCE by Babylon. A devastating military invasion by Assyria and Babylon would lead to injury, death, and destruction. The survivors would become slaves in foreign countries. The prophets intended these oracles for the nations of Israel and Judah as a whole, not for specific individuals.

This is an example of Hosea's warning of the impending invasion and destruction of Israel. The first is a threat to burn the palatial residences. The second prediction foretells their return to Egypt, where they were once enslaved. If exiled to Assyria, they would be forced to eat unclean food.

For Israel has forgotten his Maker and built palaces;

And Judah has multiplied fortified cities,

But I will send a fire on its cities that it may consume its palatial dwellings.
Hosea 8:14.

They will not remain in the Lord's land,

But Ephraim will return to Egypt,

And in Assyria they will eat unclean food. Hosea 9:3.

Some messages from God in Jeremiah and Amos provided reassurance that the Jews were under God's protection, and they would eventually return to Jerusalem.

For thus says the Lord, "When seventy years have been completed for Babylon, I will visit you and fulfill My good word to you, to bring you back to this place.

"For I know the plans that I have for you," declares the Lord, "plans for welfare and not for calamity to give you a future and a hope." Jeremiah 29:10-11

"Also I will restore the captivity of My people Israel, And they will rebuild the ruined cities and live in them;

They will also plant vineyards and drink their wine, And make gardens and eat their fruit.

"I will also plant them on their land, And they will not again be rooted out from their land

Which I have given them," Says the Lord your God. Amos 9:14-15

Many prophecies were conditional. The prophet warned the people that changing their behavior could prevent catastrophes. Here is an example from Joel.

"Yet even now," declares the Lord,

"Return to Me with all your heart,

And with fasting, weeping and mourning;

And rend your heart and not your garments."
Now return to the Lord your God,
For He is gracious and compassionate,
Slow to anger, abounding in lovingkindness
And relenting of evil. Joel 2:12-13

After a 400-year wait, John the Baptizer, Jesus' cousin, emerged. He announced the long-awaited Messiah would soon appear, followed by the Day of Judgment. He urged people to repent and to be baptized. At the start of his ministry, Jesus went to John for baptism.

Jesus had the reputation of being a prophet. During His initial ministry in Galilee, people recognized Jesus as a prophet like Elijah. He healed the sick and cast out demons. He told parables about the Kingdom of God, but people recorded few of his oracles. When He went to Jerusalem, He changed His style and delivered oracles, in particular the "woe to you..." pronouncements (Matthew 23:13-29, Luke 6:24-26, 10:13, 11:42-47, 52) and His oracle about the end times in Mark 13. While in Jerusalem, Jesus prophesied the destruction of the Temple.

Apocalyptic prophecy

A variation of prophecy is apocalyptic writing communicated from a heavenly being during a vision. Apocalypse means to reveal a secret or lift the veil. The visions predict the end of history and the triumph of good over evil. The visions are more surreal and distorted than with prophecy. They occur when severe oppression exists. Visions concern future judgment and salvation.

Malachi marked the end of the Old Testament. The genre of apocalyptic prophecies became a common form of literature during the centuries between 200 BCE and 200 CE.

Here is a comparison of prophetic and apocalyptic writing.

Prophetic

- Prophet was familiar to the people

- Oracle was public and verbal

- Scenes reflected life

- Used actual objects as symbols

- Near future

- Sun, moon, stars

Apocalyptic

- Prophet used a false name

- Oracle was written in secret and sealed

- Scenes unrealistic

- Used fantastic objects as symbols

- End of the Age

- Locusts with human heads and scorpion tails

The prophets such as Elijah, Isaiah, and Jeremiah walked among the people. Prophets using the names Baruch, Enoch, Abraham, and Moses did not reveal their identity. Jesus instructed John to leave the Book of Revelation unsealed because of its imminent fulfillment.

The prophets warned of events happening in the next few years, but apocalyptic literature predicted events at the End of the Age.

Prophets used familiar objects for their symbolism. In Joseph's dreams, the sun, moon, and stars symbolized him and his family. In contrast, John's visions in Revelation had locusts with human heads and scorpion tails.

Apocalyptic visions are present in the Old Testament books of Daniel, Ezekiel, Joel, and Zechariah. John references them when writing Revelation. The first chapter in Ezekiel recounted the prophet's vision of an immense cloud, chariots in the air, four living beings with four faces and four wings with feet like a calf's hoof. The faces were a man, a lion, a bull, and an eagle. He saw a throne with a being sitting on it surrounded by radiance.

Daniel 7:4-8 described a vision he experienced while in Babylon. Notice the four strange beasts who emerge from the sea, an apocalyptic symbol. The beasts were a lion with eagle wings, a bear with ribs in its mouth, a leopard with four heads and the wings of a bird. The fourth beast had iron teeth and ten horns; a new horn grew and displaced three of the other horns. With eyes and a mouth, the horn boasted.

In Zechariah 1:18, an angel spoke to him during a vision in which he noticed four horns that scattered the Jews. Zechariah 2:6 mentions the presence of the four winds of the heavens. Zechariah 3:9 describes a stone with seven eyes.

The Old Testament prophets connected Jerusalem with the Day of Judgment and the end times. Joel prophesied the Day of Judgment would occur in Jehoshaphat, a valley near Jerusalem (Joel 3:2). Zechariah placed it at the Mount of Olives (Zechariah 14:4).

Jesus spoke of the End of the Age in Mark 13. When the disciples asked when it would happen, He told them the signs but could not give them a date or time. He warned that the sun and moon will turn dark, and the stars will fall. There will be wars, earthquakes, famines, and floods. False prophets will deceive the followers who will face persecution and betrayal. The Son of Man will come in clouds for the Day of Judgment. He cautioned them to stay alert.

Revelation

John wrote The Book of Revelation in the 90s CE. The Christ followers suffered severe oppression from the Roman emperors. Jesus communicated with John in a series of visions and dreams. The Spirit and angels served as intermediaries.

One reason Revelation is difficult to read is its use of several literary genres. It includes apocalyptic prophecy, letters, narrative, and poetry. We will focus on apocalyptic prophecy, which includes narrative and poetry.

Let's take a minute to look at the narrative arc of the Bible before further exploring this topic. The Exposition begins with Genesis and Creation. Adam and Eve's sin and departure from the Garden serve as the Catalyst. The narratives document humanity's struggle to repent and regain their original relationship with God during the Rising Action. The Climax, or turning point, is when Jesus heads to Jerusalem to die on the cross. His followers strive to adhere to His teaching in the Falling Action after His resurrection. The Resolution is in Revelation when Satan and his minions are defeated, and Creation is restored.

Characters and settings

The book abounds in characters to carry the narrative. The main characters are the Trinity: God, Jesus, and the Holy Spirit. Characters who support them include:

- various heavenly beings,

- the four living creatures,

- saints and martyrs in heaven,

- John, the writer,

- Jesus' human followers who are still alive on earth.

The evil characters who attempt to thwart God's will are:
- Satan,

- the dragon (a symbol for Satan), the beast from the sea, and the false prophet,

- Jezebel, also called a prostitute,

- demons and fallen angels,

- Satan's human followers who are still on the earth.

Revelation includes a variety of settings for the events. A prominent setting is heaven, especially God's throne room. Earthly settings included Jerusalem, Mt. Olivet, deserts, mountains, and rivers. They also highlighted Babylon, a symbol for Rome. John knew about only the countries in the Mediterranean area, so his visions did not include other earthly locations. Settings that are introduced are the abyss, the lake of fire, the New Jerusalem, and the new Garden of Eden.

Here is a list of some of the recurring symbols in the text. Understanding these symbols gives deeper meaning to what John is trying to communicate. Using symbolism in writing urges readers to seek meanings hidden beneath the surface.

Symbol: Refers to
- Lamb, ram, lion: Jesus

- Red dragon, serpent: Satan

- Thunder, earthquakes, sea: Chaos, evil

- Sword: Judgment

- Winepress: Punishment

- Throne: Power

- Beasts from the sea: Roman empire

- Prostitute, Jezebel, Babylon: Rome

- 666: Emperor Nero

- White garments: Cleanliness, purity

- Tree: Tree of life, cross

The book of Revelation refers to Jesus as a lamb, a ram, and a lion. These images symbolize His role in the story, and we should not take them literally. Some symbols transcend cultures, such as thunder, earthquakes, or serpents.

Rome held power because of its military conquests. A symbol of Roman military strength, the cavalry wielded their swords like a scythe, making it a fearful weapon. When John wrote Jesus would overcome with the sword from His mouth (Revelation 19:15,21), this said that Jesus was in control, not Rome. Jesus both declares and implements judgment.

Here is some history about the dragon character, which symbolizes Satan. The people of that time believed in a demonic sea monster or serpent. The Canaanite serpent deities opposed the god Baal. Egypt and Babylon both have tales that mention the red dragon. The red serpent of Babylon kept watch over the god Marduk. The Jews referred to Leviathan, Rahab, and Tannin as sea monsters.[3]

Babylon was a symbol for Rome. The city was evil and corrupt during John's time. Their practice of idolatry stemmed from worshipping emperors as deities as well as the Roman gods. The Jews regarded them as immoral because of their adultery, drunkenness, greed, and lust. The upper-class lived in opulence, possessing many slaves, gold and silver, gemstones, red and purple cloth, and rare species of wood. Their military conquests enslaved more people and forced their conversion to the state religion. They tortured and executed Christians.

John's Visions

In the previous chapter, we reviewed the letters to the seven churches. Following the completion of the letters, John records a series of visions. He sees the door to heaven standing open. In the Spirit, John arrives in heaven in the Spirit, where God sits on His throne. In the throne room, angels and heavenly beings sing hymns and praise songs. John sees a slain Lamb, symbolizing Jesus. Below are some songs John recorded. The songs reference God three times and Jesus three times.

"Holy, holy, holy is the Lord God, the Almighty, who was and who is and who is to come." Revelation 4:8

And they sang a new song, saying, "Worthy are You [Jesus] to take the book and to break its seals; for You were slain, and purchased for God with Your blood men from every tribe and tongue and people and nation." Revelation 5:9

"Worthy is the Lamb that was slain to receive power and riches and wisdom and might and honor and glory and blessing." Revelation 5:12

"To Him [God] who sits on the throne, and to the Lamb, be blessing and honor and glory and dominion forever and ever." Revelation 5:13

The angels tell John about the coming judgments which eventually will culminate in the End of the Age. Visions appear one after another, in vivid color, but not always in chronological sequence.

God holds a scroll with seven seals. He hands it to the Lamb, the only one worthy to break the seals and open the scroll. With the breaking of each of the first four seals, a horseman appears. They symbolize war, famine, pestilence, and death. The breaking of the next two seals unleashes powerful storms and earthquakes. John sees a blood-red moon and stars falling to earth. There is a pause before the Lamb breaks the seventh seal.

Throughout this era, angels sound seven trumpets sequentially, each signaling devastation and loss of life.

- Hail, fire, and blood; 1/3 of earth burned

- Mountain thrown into the sea; 1/3 of sea turned to blood, 1/3 of sea creatures die

- Wormwood falls on the rivers and streams; 1/3 of the water becomes bitter and many die

- Plague of darkness; 1/3 of sun, moon, and stars turn dark

- Abyss opened, locust-scorpions emerge; harmed people without God's seal for five months

- One-third of people die; two witnesses prophesy, and are then killed

- Announcement of the End of the Age

With every trumpet call, the damage and mayhem grow more extreme. The images are disturbing. This happens for a period longer than three years.

A pause in the judgments occurs, during which the false trinity, composed of the dragon, the beast from the sea, and the false prophet, appear. The beast has ten horns, seven heads, and ten crowns on the horns. Their supporters worship the dragon and the beast, spreading lies and death.

Jesus protects his faithful followers from the harshest consequences of the judgments. According to some scholars, God gathers his followers during this pause.

The angels pour God's wrath out of seven bowls. These judgments end the punishment and destruction. They are like the plagues in Exodus, but more intense. The sixth trumpet's sound coincides with the pouring of the sixth bowl.

- Terrible sores

- Sea turns to blood

- Inland waters turn to blood

- People scorched by the sun

- Darkness (see fourth trumpet)

- Preparations by the false trinity for final battle (see sixth trumpet)

- Final battles ending current Age (concludes seventh seal, seventh trumpet)

The seventh seal, bowl, and trumpet judgments occur together and mark the End of the Age. [4] Remember, these are John's visions. We don't know whether any of these events will happen as described.

The narrative changes to the consequences for Babylon, the false trinity, and their followers. As Babylon fell, those who had profited from its wealth and luxurious commerce mourned the loss of their income. Here are laments by the kings and merchants. Notice the figurative language regarding clothing and jewels in the merchants' lament.

Lament of the Kings:

'Woe, woe, the great city, Babylon, the strong city! For in one hour your judgment has come.' Revelation 18:10

Lament of the Merchants:

'Woe, woe, the great city, she who was clothed in fine linen and purple and scarlet, and adorned with gold and precious stones and pearls;

for in one hour such great wealth has been laid waste!' Revelation 18:16-17a

The final battles with the evil characters result in the dragon, the beast, and the false prophet persecuting the faithful who remained. The false prophet pretends to be divine. Ten kings fawn over the beast's every move. Others who follow the false trinity join them. One might ask, after all this death and destruction, how could the ten kings and their armies congregate to fight? These are visions and may not be literal.

Jesus arrives on a white horse wearing a white robe dipped in blood. He is a judge and executioner. Pay particular attention to the metaphors.

His eyes are a flame of fire, and on His head are many diadems;[5] and He has a name written on Him which no one knows except Himself.

He is clothed with a robe dipped in blood, and His name is called The Word of God.

And the armies which are in heaven, clothed in fine linen, white and clean, were following Him on white horses.

From His mouth comes a sharp sword, so that with it He may strike down the nations, and He will rule them with a rod of iron; and He treads the wine press of the fierce wrath of God, the Almighty.

And on His robe and on His thigh He has a name written, "KING OF KINGS, AND LORD OF LORDS." Revelation 19:12-16

Instantly, Jesus triumphs in the battle by wielding a sword that emanates from His mouth. The beast, false prophet, and unbelievers are thrown into the lake of fire. Satan's reign ends as he is imprisoned for a millennium. During this time, Jesus rules, and peace prevails. After that time, Satan is released, revolts again, and God sends fire from above. Satan loses again and is thrown into the lake of fire. Regarding whether the thousand year reign has or will occur is hotly debated. Three schools of thought have explanations, but that is beyond the scope of this book.

In the vision, John saw that all individuals throughout history will be subject to a final judgment. God will grant rewards to individuals in the Book of Life based on their accomplishments.

In a vision, John sees that the present heaven and earth will disappear. Then, a new heaven and earth will replace them. The sea, a symbol of chaos, will no longer exist. New Jerusalem becomes a Temple for God to dwell among humanity. His radiance shines so brightly that the sun is no longer necessary.

The Spirit takes John to see New Jerusalem, the bride of the Lamb.

Then one of the seven angels ... came and spoke with me, saying, "Come here, I will show you the bride, the wife of the Lamb."

And he carried me away in the Spirit to a great and high mountain, and showed me the holy city, Jerusalem, coming down out of heaven from God, having the glory of God. Revelation 21:10-11

In New Jerusalem, there are twelve gates guarded by twelve angels. The names of the twelve apostles and twelve tribes unite all of God's people.

To celebrate their victory over Satan, God will hold a marriage banquet for all in the kingdom of heaven. The books of Isaiah, Matthew, and Luke contain the prophecy of this event. Jesus told many parables about a wedding feast.

Blessed are those who are invited to the marriage supper of the Lamb. Revelation 19:9

Blessed is everyone who will eat bread in the kingdom of God! Luke 14:15

I say to you that many will come from east and west, and recline at the table with Abraham, Isaac and Jacob in the kingdom of heaven; .... Matthew 8:11

The Lord of hosts will prepare a lavish banquet for all peoples on this mountain; .... Isaiah 25:6

The Garden of Eden descends, and the Tree of Life is available to all. From it flows the River of Life. The curse that began with Adam and Eve no longer will exist.

The Book of Revelation contains seven blessings. Those who read the book will be blessed, making it a worthwhile endeavor.

1. He who reads or hears the prophecy and heeds the contents. Revelation 1:3

2. Those who die in the Lord from the time the book was written. Revelation 14:13

3. Those who stay awake and dressed, so that they won't be naked when Christ returns. Revelation 16:15

4. Those invited to the marriage supper of Christ. Revelation 19:9

5. The one who has a part in the first resurrection. The second death is powerless, and those individuals will act as priests of God and Christ, reigning with Him for a thousand years. Revelation 20:6

6. He who pays attention to the words of this book. Revelation 22:7

7. Those who wash their robes gain entry into the city and can enjoy the tree of life. Revelation 22:14

The Book of Revelation is a fitting end to the Bible because it does the following things.

- Combines warnings from the Old and New Testament prophets with warnings from the Trinity.

- Last battles take place, and Jesus defeats Satan forever.

- Replaces the corrupt cosmos with a new heaven, new earth, and new Jerusalem.

- Restores humanity to the idyllic Garden.

This marks the end of the narrative arc found in the Bible. N. T. Wright says about the Bible:

"It is the book whose whole narrative is about new creation, that is, about resurrection, so that when the gospels each end with the raising of Jesus from the dead, and when Revelation ends with new heavens and new earth populated by God's people risen from the dead, this should not come as a surprise, but as the ultimate fulfillment of what the story had been about all along." [6]

⬦

We have reached the end of our discussion about the literary techniques present in the Bible. Familiarity with the various genres helps clarify the writer's message. The reader's understanding enhances the richness of the characters and settings in the Bible.

Through our exploration of the various literary techniques employed in the Bible, we have unearthed a rich tapestry of narratives, histories, poetry, wisdom literature, parables, letters, and visionary literature.

Exploring these diverse genres has illuminated the profound messages within the text, inviting us to not only read the words but to better understand their deeper meanings. By familiarizing ourselves with the guidelines for interpretation, we have unlocked a new level of insight and appreciation for the timeless wisdom contained within the pages of this sacred text.

May this journey of discovery continue to enrich your understanding and faith as you navigate the complexities of the Bible with newfound clarity and purpose.

If you want to dig deeper into this topic, I suggest the References following each chapter.

Reflect on the literary form of the Bible when you next read it, considering its contribution to the story. I hope that by gaining a deeper understanding, the reader will come to appreciate the Bible's richness.

---

1. Ben Witherington, III, *Jesus the Seer: The Progress of Prophecy*. Peabody, (MA: Hendrickson Publishers, Inc., 1999) 269.

2. Fee, 182.

3. Leviathan (Job 3:8; 41:1, Psalm 74:13–14, 104:26); Rahab (Job 9:13; 26:12; Isaiah 51:9); Tannin (Job 7:12; Psalm 74:13).

4. Grant R. Osborne, *Revelation Verse by Verse*, Osborne New Testament Commentaries, (Bellingham, WA: Lexham Press 2016), 273.

5. Royal crowns.

6. N. T. Wright, *Surprised by Hope*, (London: Society for Promoting Christian Knowledge, 2007) 295.

References

Bartholomew, Craig G. *When You Want to Yell at God: The Book of Job*, ed. Craig G. Bartholomew et al., Transformative Word. Bellingham, WA: Lexham Press, 2014.

Beck, John A. *Along the Road: How Jesus Used Geography to Tell God's Story*. Grand Rapids, MI: Discovery House, 2018.

Fee, Gordon D., and Douglas K. Stuart. *How to Read the Bible for All Its Worth*. 3rd ed. Grand Rapids, MI: Zondervan, 2003.

New American Standard Bible: 1995 Update. La Habra, CA: The Lockman Foundation, 1995.

Osborne, Grant R. *Revelation Verse by Verse*. Osborne New Testament Commentaries. Bellingham, WA: Lexham Press, 2016.

Ryken, Leland. *How to Read the Bible as Literature*. Grand Rapids, MI: Zondervan, 1984.

Siker, Judy Yates, and Patricia Lynn Miller. *Who is Jesus? What a Difference a Lens Makes*. Horizons Presbyterian Women, Inc. Presbyterian Church USA, 2016.

Smith, James E. *The Major Prophets*. Old Testament Survey Series. Joplin, MO: College Press, 1992.

Smith, James E. *The Wisdom Literature and Psalms*. Old Testament Survey Series. Joplin, MO: College Press Pub. Co., 1996.

Wiersbe, Warren W. *Be Committed*. "Be" Commentary Series. Wheaton, IL: Victor Books, 1993.

Witherington, Ben III. *Jesus the Seer: The Progress of Prophecy.* Peabody, MA: Hendrickson Publishers, Inc., 1999.

Wright, N. T. *Surprised by Hope.* London: Society for Promoting Christian Knowledge, 2007.